HACK YOUR CUPBOARD

Make Great Food with What You've Got

ALYSSA WIEGAND & CARLA CARREON

ZEST BOOKS
MINNEAPOLIS

CONTENTS

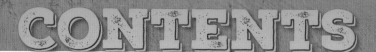

INTRODUCTION

Who We Are (and Were)

Do you watch cooking shows and wish you could cook like that? You totally can. It just takes a little practice and help! We're Alyssa and Carla, and we love to eat, cook, and show others how to do it themselves.

This is Alyssa. Her cooking attire has changed slightly over the years, but she still loves to sneak tastes straight from the bowl. She loves to throw dinner parties, but hates doing the dishes afterward. She can't get enough carbs – bring on the pasta and bread! Her personal cooking philosophy is: "Everything is better with cheese."

This is Carla. She's the youngest of four girls, so she grew up doing a lot of dishes and prep work. (You should see her chop vegetables!) She makes a mean hash brown and is currently finding as many recipes as possible that allow her to bake with lemons. In the kitchen, you're most likely to find her roasting vegetables or putting cinnamon sugar on everything from toast to carrots.

Why We Wrote This Book

We wrote this book because we wanted to show people how easy it is to cook great-tasting food for yourself and your favorite people. We both happened to grow up in large families with some killer cooking role models, but we still had to learn how to upgrade from pouring our own bowls of cereal to mastering a few recipes. If you're still at the cereal-for-dinner stage, that's okay! It's a start!

One of the most important concepts in this book is the idea of "hacking" your recipes and using what you have on hand. Hacking involves thinking about what you like to eat and how it might improve the dish you're cooking – think of every recipe like a make-your-own pizza. Is there something in your pantry you could add?

In addition to recipe hacks, this book will teach you about ingredients, tools, and techniques. These sections will help you feel comfortable in the kitchen and grow your skills so that you can get from simple sandwiches and toast to fancy main courses like braised pork. The ultimate goal is for you to be able to figure out and cook exactly what you want in any kitchen.

How the Book Is Organized

Hack Your Cupboard guides you through some important living (and cooking) situations. There are four major sections for each kind of kitchen you might encounter. "Your First Kitchen" is all about getting started, "Dorm Room Dining" helps you prepare meals and snacks with little more than a microwave, "First Apartment Dining" helps you navigate a shared kitchen with roommates, and "First Solo Kitchen" helps you get set up on your own. These sections also include:

Pantry guidelines: Talking about pantries is a big task, particularly when you're working in someone else's kitchen. Ingredients can vary wildly based on many things, including culture, region of the country, and even the time of year. While we hope our pantry guides capture most of the foods you're used to eating, be prepared for some differences. When you're trying out recipes, just make sure that you have the right ingredients — it's pretty sad to get excited about making avocado toast . . . and then find out you have zero avocados.

Equipment suggestions: In these sections, we talk about the tools that you might have in your kitchen, plus the ones you might want to buy. Your first kitchen is probably the one you have at home, but it could also be a grandparent's kitchen, a kitchen at school, or even your friend's kitchen! If you don't have all the items we describe, don't worry — you can often improvise. Beyond that, start making a list of anything you might want to add to your collection. You can also check dollar stores and garage sales for inexpensive tools.

Knife skills: There are two knife-skill sections in this book, intended to help you get through any recipe you might encounter. We cover skills like knife holding, and we explain several different types of cuts.

Recipes, techniques, and hacks: We combine techniques with recipes that let you practice new skills right away. Look for the suggested hacks at the end of each recipe to help you take them to the next level. Some of the hacks we came up with include spicy hacks to add a little kick, gourmet hacks to trick out your dish, or fun hacks to add a little color to your day.

A party menu: Sharing your food with others is one of the best parts about cooking (and everyone loves a party)! Each section comes with a party menu using recipes that you just learned, but don't forget to add your own hacks and favorite recipes. You be you!

Tips and tricks: Peppered within each section (pun intended), you'll find lots of helpful information, including safety tips, spice ideas, budget tricks, and more.

Fun in the kitchen really begins once you know that ingredients are flexible, as long as you have solid techniques and the right tools. This opens up a whole new world of cooking and hacking recipes or dishes. Experimenting with new flavors and combinations gives you independence and freedom.

Don't Skip Over

a section if it doesn't apply to you! You'll still find great recipes and tips that you might not already know.

How to Read the Recipes

While we love hacking recipes, even the most seasoned cooks need to be prepared when approaching a new dish. Before you start cooking any recipe, it's important to take the time to read through the ingredient list and the recipe itself. It's never fun to get ready to make spaghetti and then discover that you don't have pasta or you didn't prep the tomatoes properly. Taking a minute to read through the recipe also gives you a chance to look up any terms you're unfamiliar with and maybe watch an online video about a technique with which you may not be comfortable.

Follow these steps for each recipe:

1. Make sure you have all of the ingredients.

2. Look for any hidden instructions in the ingredient list. Recipes can be sneaky! If a recipe says "1 onion, chopped," you should chop the onion and set it aside. If you missed the "chopped" part, you might just throw a whole onion in the pot!

3. Get out all of your ingredients, measure them out, and do any prep work. (As you learn how to hack recipes, you'll also want to prepare your substitutions or additions now.)

4. Assemble any equipment you might need, and have it within easy reach.

5. Start following the recipe itself! Good luck!

Other tips

Did you know that the commas and word order in ingredient lists are very carefully placed? There is a difference between "1 cup peanuts, chopped" and "1 cup chopped peanuts," and sometimes this interpretation can really change the flavor or texture of a recipe. In the first example, you measure out 1 cup of peanuts and then chop them. In the second example, you chop a bunch of peanuts, then measure out 1 cup. You can fit a lot more peanuts in 1 cup when they're already chopped up, so watch those commas!

Look for certain buzzwords when baking. For example, you may need "2 eggs, separated." This means that you separate the egg whites from the yolks, and usually you will add them to the recipe at different times. Other words or phrases to look for: *softened*, *at room temperature*, *melted*, *sifted*, *packed*.

Cook times vary slightly based on differences from kitchen to kitchen, so almost every recipe will give you a range of time for how long steps take or when the dish is done. Start checking the food at the beginning of the time suggested, and pay attention to visual clues and smells that indicate it's done – that the onions are translucent or the cookies are golden brown. Many times, the recipe will even tell you what to look for.

If the recipe doesn't have a list of equipment, it might be helpful to make one as you read through the recipe. Take out all of the equipment in advance.

Don't be afraid to add your own notes as well! You'll be able to refer to them later to make the dish better each time you make it. If you'd rather not write in the book, use sticky notes instead.

YOUR FIRST KITCHEN

Learning to cook can seem like a big project, but all it takes to get started is a kitchen and a willingness to try. This section is all about familiarizing yourself with the first kitchen to which you have access, no matter where that happens to be. You'll learn some new skills, cook some easy recipes, and try your hand at hacking some dishes.

First Kitchen Pantry

A well-stocked pantry is important for healthy, homemade meals. Based on your cultural heritage, where you live, and how your family eats, your pantry might vary from this list. Don't be discouraged if that's the case; look at it as a fun way to get your family to try new ingredients and recipes and as an opportunity to practice your hacking skills! To get started, this section's recipes use the following pantry staples:

EXTRA VIRGIN OLIVE OIL
A flavorful oil commonly used in salad dressings, cooking, and baking.

COOKING OIL (SUCH AS CANOLA OR SAFFLOWER)
A neutral oil that holds up to high cooking temperatures. Can be used in place of olive oil.

NONSTICK COOKING SPRAY
Used in baking and to keep roasted items from sticking to the pan.

ALL-PURPOSE FLOUR AND SUGAR (GRANULATED AND LIGHT BROWN)
Flour and sugar are critical components in baking and in certain savory-dish techniques.

CANNED TOMATOES
Canned tomatoes add flavor, color, and bulk to soups, chilis, and sauces.

PASTA
Dried pasta comes in many shapes and is made easily with just boiling water.

VINEGAR (BALSAMIC, RED WINE, OR WHITE WINE)
A key ingredient in homemade salad dressings, vinegar adds acidity and flavor to recipes.

GARLIC
Cloves of garlic are an aromatic ingredient present in recipes from around the world.

SALT AND PEPPER
The simplest way to begin seasoning your dishes.

ITALIAN SEASONING
A blend of different dried herbs, Italian seasoning usually contains dried basil, oregano, rosemary, and marjoram.

VANILLA EXTRACT
In addition to being a delicious flavor on its own, vanilla extract also enhances the flavors of other ingredients, such as chocolate or fruit.

BAKING SODA AND BAKING POWDER
Baking soda and baking powder are ingredients that help baked goods rise.

First Kitchen Equipment

Kitchens are often stocked with basic cooking essentials, such as pots and pans, measuring cups and spoons, mixing bowls, and cooking utensils. Some specific tools mentioned in this chapter include:

KNIVES
Your family's kitchen will likely have a knife set with differently sized knives. The chef's knife is the most versatile and is featured in our Knife Skills section on page 23.

CUTTING BOARD
When using a knife, use a cutting board for safety and to protect your counters.

GARLIC PRESS
A garlic press crushes cloves, making the use of fresh garlic in your recipes a breeze.

SPATULAS, WOODEN SPOONS, AND TONGS
These tools are essential for handling and serving food.

COLANDER
This tool is used to drain food and makes it easy to wash produce.

BAKING SHEETS
These metal sheets are used in the oven for baking and roasting.

Hacking Your Family's Pantry

To get started, here's a simple meal to help you see how easy it can be to hack any dish. Begin by making your favorite packaged macaroni and cheese. Whether you're preparing the boxed version or a microwavable bowl, use the recipe-reading tips on page 9 to help you follow the instructions.

Now let's hack the dish! Look at the chart below, and check your cupboard for the ingredients you have on hand that can be mixed in. Some may need to be cooked first, as indicated by the asterisk. (Use leftovers or precooked frozen or canned versions when you can.)

PROTEIN	VEGGIES	SAUCY MIX-INS	SPICES	TOPPINGS
bacon*	broccoli*	salsa	pepper	more cheese!
chicken*	mushrooms*	pizza sauce	chili powder	breadcrumbs
ground beef or taco meat*	spinach	alfredo sauce	cumin powder	crumbled crackers
ham*	canned peppers	mustard	Italian seasoning	avocado
black beans*	peas*	cream cheese	red pepper flakes	green onions
turkey*	onions*	hot sauce	garlic or onion powder	fried egg
pepperoni	jalapeños (canned or pickled)			
sausage*	olives			
vegetarian meat substitute*	fresh tomatoes			

* These items need to be cooked first!

Some of our favorite combos include:

Broccoli + cream cheese + breadcrumbs

Sausage + black beans + cumin powder + avocado

Pepperoni + mushrooms + pizza sauce

Bacon + sliced tomatoes + fried egg + avocado

Beginner Techniques and Recipes

SALADS AND VINAIGRETTES

It's not hard to make a basic salad. But salads are the perfect start to hacking recipes because there are so many different ingredients you can use, from the type of lettuce to the dressing to the toppings. Salads can be so much tastier and healthier than iceberg lettuce swimming in store-bought dressing.

Making your own salad dressing is incredibly easy with just a few pantry ingredients. On top of how simple it is, creating your own dressing is delicious and fun. We love knowing the ingredients that are going into our dressings — basic vinaigrettes are just olive oil, vinegar, and a bit of salt and pepper. Once you've mastered the concept, you can experiment with herbs and spices, different kinds of juices or oils, and adding ingredients like mustard or sour cream to make them creamier.

HOW TO MAKE A PERFECT VINAIGRETTE:

Three easy steps are crucial to making the perfect salad.

Ratio: When making your vinaigrette, start with a ratio of 1 part vinegar to 2 parts oil. This means that for every tablespoon of vinegar, you add 2 tablespoons of oil. You can then adjust this based on your personal taste and the ingredients you use. Certain ingredients, like balsamic vinegar or orange juice, are less acidic and you can use more of them in the dressing. Others, like red wine vinegar or lemon juice, are very tart and can overwhelm the dressing if you use too much.

Emulsification: Oil doesn't mix well with most other liquids, so you have to force them together through a process called emulsification. Many recipes or cookbooks will tell you to slowly add oil to vinegar, whisking to emulsify. A much easier method is to combine all of your dressing ingredients in a small, airtight container like a mason jar or a clean jam jar, and shake the jar vigorously for about 15 seconds. You'll have a perfectly combined dressing! Taste a leaf of lettuce with a touch of the dressing to see how it will taste on the salad. Now you can adjust the ratio if your dressing is too acidic or too oily.

Dressing the greens: Put the clean, dry greens in a large bowl — one that looks way too big for the salad. Drizzle a little bit of dressing over the greens, and use your clean hands to gently toss them in the dressing. Try a leaf to make sure you can actually taste the dressing. Keep adding dressing a little bit at a time until you're happy with the flavor. Don't add so much that the greens are sitting in a pool of dressing, or you won't taste the lettuce. It's important to wait until just before eating to dress the greens to avoid wilted lettuce.

Tips

You can store dressing made from oil and vinegar in an airtight container for up to two weeks. If you used juice, fresh herbs, or any other perishable ingredients, refrigerate the dressing for up to four days, but try to use it very quickly for the best flavor.

Shake the jar well before using, as your oil and acid will have separated. You'll need 2 tablespoons of dressing for each 2-cup serving of lettuce.

Basic Vinaigrettes

RED WINE VINAIGRETTE

Makes 2 servings.

INGREDIENTS
1 tablespoon red wine vinegar
3 tablespoons extra virgin olive oil
½ teaspoon kosher sea salt
¼ teaspoon freshly cracked pepper

BALSAMIC VINAIGRETTE

Makes 2 servings.

INGREDIENTS
2 tablespoons balsamic vinegar
2 tablespoons extra virgin olive oil
½ teaspoon kosher sea salt
¼ teaspoon freshly cracked pepper

LEMON AND OREGANO VINAIGRETTE

Makes 2 servings.

INGREDIENTS
1 tablespoon freshly squeezed lemon juice
  (from about half a lemon)
3 tablespoons extra virgin olive oil
1 teaspoon oregano
½ teaspoon kosher sea salt
¼ teaspoon freshly cracked pepper

STEPS FOR ALL RECIPES ABOVE:

1. Combine the ingredients in the airtight container.

2. Seal and shake for about 15 seconds to combine the ingredients.

3. Taste, and adjust salt and pepper as necessary.

GREEK SALAD

Makes 2 servings.

INGREDIENTS
4 cups baby spinach
1 recipe lemon and oregano vinaigrette (page 17)
1 cup halved cherry tomatoes
½ hothouse or English cucumber, cut into ¼-inch slices
⅓ cup crumbled feta cheese
⅓ cup pitted Kalamata olives, cut into quarters
⅛ red onion, sliced thin

STEPS
1. Wash the greens in a colander and thoroughly dry them. You can air dry them, or use a clean towel or a salad spinner to speed up the process.

2. Place the greens in a large bowl. Add a little bit of the dressing, and use your hands to gently coat the greens in the dressing. Add more dressing until the greens are lightly coated.

3. Taste, and adjust salt and pepper as necessary.

4. Add the cherry tomato halves, cucumber slices, feta cheese, Kalamata olives, and red onion slices. Toss to combine.

HEARTY HACK
Add grilled chicken or shrimp to turn this salad into a full meal.

GOURMET HACK
Marinate the cucumbers and tomatoes in 1 tablespoon of salad dressing 30 minutes before serving.

One of the beautiful things about salads is that you can put anything in them!

Here are some of our favorite toppings:
- sunflower seeds, croutons, tortilla strips, black beans, shredded carrot
- hard-boiled or fried eggs, cheese (any kind), fresh or dried fruit
- grilled or roasted vegetables, like peppers, zucchini, and potatoes
- fresh herbs, like mint, parsley, cilantro, and basil

Amazing Scrambled Eggs

Eggs can be a meal by themselves, or they can contribute to dishes in ways both seen and unseen. Fried or poached eggs can add richness to salads, soups, pizzas, pasta, and sandwiches. They're included in almost every baking recipe, and they act as a binder for many fried foods. You can start learning how to cook with them by making an underrated breakfast dish: scrambled eggs.

Eggs are full of protein, and protein becomes tough when overcooked. (Have you ever had rubbery scrambled eggs? They were probably cooked for too long over too-high heat.) This recipe gently cooks the eggs so they stay tender, light, and fluffy.

BASIC SCRAMBLED EGGS

Makes 1 serving.

INGREDIENTS
2 large eggs
1 tablespoon milk
½ tablespoon water
¼ teaspoon sea salt
¼ teaspoon freshly ground pepper
½ tablespoon butter

COOKING FOR A CROWD

This recipe is easily adaptable for a larger group. Assume 2–3 eggs per person, and multiply the ingredients accordingly. Allow a few extra minutes to cook the additional eggs in step 3.

STEPS

1. Crack the eggs into a medium-sized bowl. Add the milk, water, salt, and pepper to the bowl. Whisk to combine the ingredients.

2. Heat a nonstick skillet over medium-low heat. Add the butter, and swirl it around in the pan until it melts and coats the pan.

3. Add the egg mixture and let it cook for 60–90 seconds, until a thin layer has cooked on the bottom of the pan. You should start to see a bit of steam rising from the eggs. If there is a lot of steam or even smoke, remove the pan from the heat. Reduce the temperature to low to prevent overcooking. Use your spatula to gently push the cooked layer over to one side of the pan, letting the uncooked egg run onto the pan. Repeat until there is no more liquid egg. This should take about 3 minutes total.

4. Turn off the heat and use the spatula to break up any large pieces of egg. Gently stir the eggs to make sure they're cooked and aren't too wet.

5. Taste, and adjust salt and pepper as needed.

CHEESY SCRAMBLED EGGS

Melted cheese can transform scrambled eggs from a good breakfast into an amazing start to the morning. Simply add ⅛ cup shredded or crumbled cheese in the Basic Scrambled Eggs recipe, right after step 3. Our favorites are cheeses that melt easily, such as cheddar, mozzarella, fresh goat cheese, and any Mexican or Italian cheese blends.

Once you've mastered the basic technique, it's easy to add your favorite ingredients to make your own signature scrambled eggs. They're also the perfect way to use up leftovers from the refrigerator: the onion for which you don't have any plans, or that small piece of cheddar cheese that you didn't use in last night's recipe. However, most ingredients need to be cooked before you add them to the eggs, because scrambled eggs have such a short cooking time and cook over lower heat (cheese is the only exception, as you can add it directly to the eggs). Use the same pan to cook your add-ins first, then remove them, wipe the pan clean, and start with an empty pan for your eggs. Add the extra ingredients to the recipe at the beginning of step 4, so that they become incorporated into the eggs as you gently stir them.

Some of our favorite scrambled egg combinations are:

- Roasted potatoes, roasted red peppers, and mozzarella cheese
- Caramelized onions (page 102), sautéed mushrooms, and Gruyère cheese
- Crisped bacon, cooked sausage, and cheddar cheese
- Fresh baby spinach, halved cherry tomatoes, and feta cheese
- Cooked ground beef, sautéed onions, and a Mexican cheese blend
- Chopped chives and fresh goat cheese

First Kitchen Knife Skills

We're about to use a knife, so let's go over some basic skills. (Don't be nervous; you've got this!) A sharp knife will make cooking more fun and will actually make you less likely to cut yourself! If you notice that your knives are getting dull, we recommend taking them to be professionally sharpened. Many kitchen-supply stores and hardware stores offer the service, and you can sometimes find vendors at farmers' markets who will sharpen your knives on the spot.

How to Hold and Use a Chef's Knife

It may seem counterintuitive, but you want to have a firm hold on the blade itself when using a chef's knife. Obviously, you don't put your fingers near the sharp edge, but your thumb and forefinger will actually touch the blade. Start by gripping the handle of the knife with your middle, ring, and pinky fingers, with your palm near where the handle meets the blade. The knuckle of your index finger will be on the top of the blade. Now place your thumb on the side of the blade, with the tip of your thumb pointing toward the tip of the knife. Place your index finger on the opposite side of the blade from your thumb, and bend it back so that the tip of your finger is pointing toward the handle. All of your fingers should be tucked out of the way now, and you should have a solid grip on the knife. This grip will give you more control over the knife than if you were to grip only the handle.

When using a chef's knife, make sure you tuck away the fingers of your other hand! Make a claw and grip the food with your fingertips. Your knuckles should actually be closer to the knife than your fingertips are. This way, if your blade touches any part of the other hand, it will just be the side of the blade touching your knuckles. No harm done!

How to Slice

When a recipe calls for sliced food, it usually specifies how thick the slices need to be. Cut the food into thin pieces of a uniform size.

How to Julienne and Chop

Start by slicing your food into long planks about ¼-inch thick. For very long objects, such as carrots, zucchinis, or cucumbers, you will cut the item into several sections of no more than 4 to 5 inches long. If your recipe calls for a certain size julienne, cut the lengths of your item into the specified measurement.

Stack your planks and cut them into a matchstick shape, about ¼-inch thick again. You may not be able to cut through all of the planks neatly, so you can do two or three at a time to make sure they're all the same size. Now you have a julienne, or matchstick!

To chop your food, stack your matchsticks into a neat bundle with the edges lined up, and cut off small squares. You've chopped your food!

Chop, Dice, or Mince?

Sometimes recipes will call for a diced or minced ingredient. What's the difference?

Chop: About ¼-inch pieces, commonly used for vegetables when you want them to still be intact at the end of cooking.

Dice: About ⅛-inch pieces, commonly used for vegetables when you want them to disappear into the dish by the end of cooking.

Mince: Make the pieces as small as you can with your knife. This is commonly used for garlic, shallots, and herbs.

How to Chop an Onion

Onions and shallots are a little harder to chop, because they have concentric rings that will fall apart as you cut them. You have to treat them differently to make sure you end up with similarly sized pieces that will cook uniformly.

The onion has a root end (which looks almost hairy), a stem end (which can look like a tail), and is covered in an inedible, papery skin.

Start by cutting off the stem end to create a flat edge. Place the onion cut-side down on the cutting board. Now cut the onion in half through the root end. Peel off the papery skin.

Place half of the onion on the cutting board, with the round side facing up. Leave the root end intact, and use it to hold the onion together until you're done chopping it. Cut horizontally into the onion two or three times, stopping just short of the root end (don't cut all the way through!). Be careful to keep your fingers out of the way of the knife! Repeat with the other half.

Slice vertically into the onion, leaving about ¼ inch between slices. Don't cut through the root end yet!

Cut across the onion in ¼-inch slices, stopping just before you get to the root end. Discard the root. The onion should fall onto your cutting board in small squares as you chop.

Toast

Do you know the phrase "the best thing since sliced bread"? Well, it exists because sliced bread is pretty amazing. Toast is one of the easiest and most versatile foods that you can possibly make. Nearly every culture has its own version of toasted bread, making it a comforting, soul-satisfying dish no matter where you're from. Let's talk toast and look at some different ways to make sliced bread even better.

AVOCADO TOAST

Something magical happens when you combine ripe avocados with crusty, lightly toasted bread. Keep it simple or dress it up with different flavor combinations, and enjoy it for breakfast, lunch, or dinner.

Look for avocados that are darker and more of a purple-black color. Green avocados are generally underripe. When you pick it up, the flesh should yield slightly to pressure. A hard avocado is underripe, will taste green, and won't have the characteristically creamy texture of avocados. If it feels very soft, it's overripe and will be mushy, brown, and taste like dirt. Never buy overripe avocados, but if you need to buy underripe avocados, you can place them in a brown paper bag and let them sit at room temperature for three to six days.

Avocados have an unusual shape and construction, so you need to be a little creative to prepare them. The skin is inedible, and there is a large, hard pit in the center of the fruit. Here are the steps for getting to the creamy flesh:

- Carefully slice into the avocado lengthwise with a sharp chef's knife, stopping when you hit the pit. Rotate your knife all the way around the pit, cutting the avocado into two halves.

- Separate the halves by twisting in opposite directions. The pit will stick in one half.

- Hold the half with the pit in your nondominant hand. Hold the knife in your other hand, and firmly but quickly stick the blade into the pit, so that it becomes impaled on the knife. Twist the knife to remove the pit.

- Do NOT remove the pit by grabbing it with your hand! Hold the knife on a cutting board with the pit and sharp edge facing down. Place the forefinger and thumb of your other hand over the top of the blade (the dull edge) and carefully pinch the pit toward the cutting board, off the knife.

- Gently run a large spoon between the avocado flesh and the skin. Remove the flesh. Discard the pit and skin.

SLICED AVOCADO TOAST WITH OLIVE OIL

Makes 4 servings.

INGREDIENTS
2 ripe avocados
4 lightly toasted pieces of your favorite sliced bread
2 tablespoons high-quality extra virgin olive oil
½ teaspoon sea salt
Fresh pepper

STEPS

1. Prepare the avocado according to the instructions on page 27.

2. Cut the avocado flesh lengthwise into ½-inch slices.

3. Divide the avocado slices among your toast. Drizzle each piece of toast with ½ tablespoon of olive oil, and sprinkle with a pinch of salt and a crack of fresh pepper.

SPICY HACK

Add a few drops of your favorite hot sauce or a shake of red pepper flakes.

Avocados

Avocado flesh turns brown when exposed to oxygen, so try to cut avocados just before serving. If you need to save cut avocados, spread some lime juice, lemon juice, or oil onto the flesh to prevent oxidation. You can also leave the pit in to minimize the flesh's contact with the air.

MASHED AVOCADO TOAST WITH GARLIC AND LIME

Makes 4 servings.

INGREDIENTS
2 ripe avocados
4 lightly toasted pieces of your favorite sliced bread
1 teaspoon freshly squeezed lime juice (from about half of a lime)
1 clove garlic, peeled and cut in half
½ teaspoon sea salt
2 turns of fresh pepper from a pepper mill

GOURMET HACK
Add a sprinkle of chopped cilantro and/or a drizzle of fresh extra virgin olive oil. Add a fried egg (page 108).

STEPS
1. When the bread is fresh out of the toaster or oven, gently rub the cut end of the garlic halves on one side of the toast.

2. Cut the avocado flesh into ½-inch cubes. Transfer to a medium bowl, and mash with a fork until only slightly chunky. Add lime juice and salt. Mix well.

3. Divide the mashed avocado among your toasted bread, spreading evenly over the side with the garlic. Top with a twist of freshly ground pepper.

Grilled Cheese

Now that we've established what a great base toast makes for other ingredients, you can start to experiment with grilled cheese. At its simplest, a grilled cheese sandwich is really just two pieces of toast with melted cheese (and maybe other delicious goodies) between them. Here's an introduction to making gooey, crispy grilled cheese sandwiches. You can use virtually any kind of bread or cheese, in any combination that you like, as long as you have the basic technique down.

BASIC GRILLED CHEESE SANDWICH

Makes 1 serving.

INGREDIENTS
2 slices bread, about ½-inch thick
About 2 tablespoons spreadable butter
2 slices cheese, or about 1½ ounces cheese

STEPS
1. Heat frying pan over medium heat.

2. Lightly butter both sides of the bread slices.

3. Toast one side of each of the bread slices on the frying pan until golden brown (2-3 minutes).

4. Flip the bread so the toasted side is facing up in the frying pan. Place the cheese on one slice of bread. Top with the other slice of bread, with the toasted side on the inside and the untoasted side facing up.

5. Toast until the bottom slice is golden brown (2-3 minutes).

6. When the bottom is golden, use a spatula to flip the sandwich and toast the final side until golden brown (2-3 minutes). Remove from the heat.

7. Cut the sandwiches into quarters and eat!

We feel very strongly about toasting both sides of the bread for maximum buttery, toasty goodness, but we know that you may not always want to take the time. If necessary, you can skip steps 3 and 4. Just make a sandwich and toast each side if you're short on time.

The recipes on the next few pages use the basic technique outlined above, but they have a little bit of a gourmet twist.

GOURMET HACK

Combine different cheeses, such as cheddar + Swiss, pepper jack + provolone, or mozzarella + Parmesan + ricotta.

PEPPERONI GRILLED CHEESE

Makes 1 serving.

INGREDIENTS
2 slices Italian or French bread, cut about ½-inch thick
About 2 tablespoons spreadable butter
About 1½ ounces shredded or sliced mozzarella cheese
6 slices pepperoni
¼ teaspoon Italian seasoning
Optional: ¼ cup pizza sauce for dipping

STEPS

1. Toss the mozzarella cheese with the Italian seasoning.

2. Follow the steps on page 31, layering pepperoni on top of the cheese in step 4.

3. If using pizza sauce, microwave over medium heat for about 2 minutes, stirring often, until sauce is warm.

4. Cut the sandwich into quarters and dip in the pizza sauce.

BRIE AND JAM GRILLED CHEESE

Makes 1 serving.

INGREDIENTS

2 slices Italian or French bread, about ½-inch thick
About 1 tablespoon spreadable butter
1 ounce of Brie cheese, cut into ¼-ounce pieces
½ tablespoon your favorite fruit jam, such as
**   fig or apricot**

STEPS

1. Heat frying pan over medium heat for about 5 minutes.

2. Lightly butter both sides of the bread slices.

3. Toast one side of each of the bread slices on the frying pan until golden brown (2–3 minutes).

4. Flip the bread so the toasted side is facing up in the frying pan. Spread the Brie on one of the toasted sides of bread, and spread the jam on the toasted side of the second slice of bread. Sandwich the cheese and jam pieces together.

5. Toast until the bottom slice is golden brown (2–3 minutes).

6. When the bottom is golden, use a spatula to flip the sandwich and toast the final side until golden brown (2–3 minutes). Remove from the heat.

7. Cut the sandwiches into quarters and enjoy!

GOURMET HACK

Gourmet hack: Add slices of apples or chopped nuts with the cheese in step 4.

What kind of cheese should I use?

Perfect for grilled cheese (because they melt easily):

American, cheddar, pepper jack, Gruyère, Swiss, Brie, Havarti, provolone, Muenster, mozzarella

Great when paired with a melty cheese:

Parmesan (and other hard cheeses), feta, blue cheese, fresh goat cheese, ricotta

How to Cook Pasta

Pasta makes an affordable, satisfying, and delicious meal. It's incredibly versatile, and you can make it as simple or as elaborate as you like. Some of the best pasta dishes don't have a "sauce" at all, but are simply noodles lightly coated in olive oil or butter and seasoned with grated cheese, salt, and pepper.

Pasta also comes in a variety of shapes. Small shapes, such as orzo or stelline, are perfect in soups and broth. Heartier pastas like penne and rotini are designed to catch chunkier sauces in their crevices. Long, thin shapes such as spaghetti, linguine, and angel hair (capellini) are best with smoother sauces like marinara or alfredo.

Making sauce from scratch is a rewarding process, but there are plenty of canned sauce options that you can keep in your pantry in case you need a quick weeknight meal. You can easily doctor canned sauce with a drizzle of balsamic vinegar, a dash of Italian seasoning, a pinch of red pepper flakes, or a sprinkle of freshly grated Parmesan cheese.

The term for properly cooked pasta is *al dente*, which is Italian for "to the tooth." It means that you meet slight resistance when biting into the pasta. The noodles shouldn't be mushy, but they also shouldn't have any crunch to them. People claim to use some interesting methods to tell them when pasta is done (such as throwing a noodle against a wall to see if it sticks!), but the only way to truly tell is to taste it. Most pasta packaging indicates how long you need to cook the noodles to have them reach this perfect al dente state.

Draining Pasta

When draining pasta, be sure to pour out the water and pasta slowly. You want to avoid flooding the sink, which can transfer any germs or bacteria from the drain or sink to the colander and, ultimately, to your pasta. An ideal colander can be suspended completely above the sink, or it has a pedestal to keep it raised above the sink bottom to prevent the water from backing up into the colander.

Basic Pasta Preparation

Makes 4 generous servings.

INGREDIENTS
1 package dried pasta (about 12-16 ounces)
1 tablespoon salt

STEPS

1. Fill a large pot with about 5 quarts of water. Add the salt. Bring the water to a boil over high heat.

2. Check the pasta's packaging to see how long you need to cook it.

3. Place a colander in the sink.

4. Once the water is at a rolling boil, add the pasta. Stir often with a wooden spoon for as long as the package indicates. If the water starts to boil over, reduce the heat to medium-high.

5. When you've reached the amount of time indicated on the package, remove a piece of pasta from the water with the wooden spoon and let it cool slightly on a small plate. Taste it to see if it is al dente (see page 36 for description).

6. Pour the water and the pasta into the colander set in the sink. Drain the pasta and return to the pot. Don't worry about making sure all the water is removed from the noodles.

Reserving Pasta Water

Pasta releases starch into the water while it cooks. Some recipes call for a little bit of reserved cooking water, which takes advantage of this starch to make the sauce creamier.

A QUICK TIP: It's a habit for most people to drain all the water down the sink, forgetting to reserve the pasta water. Oops! Set your measuring cup in the colander so you can't drain the pasta without seeing the measuring cup; this will remind you to reserve the water.

PENNE WITH MARINARA SAUCE

Makes 4 servings.

INGREDIENTS
4 tablespoons extra virgin olive oil
3 tablespoons butter
4 cloves garlic, peeled and crushed (but still intact)
2 14.5-ounce cans petite diced tomatoes
1 teaspoon salt
1 teaspoon Italian seasoning
½ teaspoon red pepper flakes
12 ounces dried penne pasta
Optional: ½ cup grated Italian cheese for serving

GOURMET HACK

Add a few tablespoons of chopped basil just before serving.

STEPS

1. Heat a nonstick skillet over medium heat. Add the olive oil and butter and heat for 30 seconds, until the butter melts.

2. Peel the papery skin off the garlic and crush it gently. Swirl to coat the pan with olive oil. Add the garlic and cloves, letting them infuse the butter and oil with flavor. Cook until garlic turns golden brown (about 8–10 minutes). Remove the garlic and discard.

3. Once the garlic is done, add the tomatoes and their juices to the pan. Add the salt, Italian seasoning, and red pepper flakes. Stir well with a wooden spoon. Let the tomatoes simmer over medium heat for about 10 minutes, stirring often.

4. Meanwhile, cook the penne according to the instructions on page 37.

5. After you drain the penne, return it to the pot and add the tomato sauce. Toss to coat.

How to Crush Garlic

Slice off the hard end of the garlic, leaving the pointy end intact and the papery skin on. Hold your chef's knife so that the side of the blade sandwiches the garlic against the cutting board, toward the center-top of the knife. The sharp edge of the blade should be angled down against the cutting board, so it can't cut you. Use the palm of your free hand to push down the side of the blade, and smash the garlic between the knife and the cutting board. The papery skin should fall off, and the clove should be fairly intact but crushed.

CACIO E PEPE

Cacio e pepe is Italian for "cheese and pepper." In English, we call it cheese and black pepper spaghetti. In any language, this is a simple combination of ingredients that creates delicious pasta. For best results, use a block of fresh cheese and grate it yourself. Look for Parmesan or Pecorino Romano in your grocery store's gourmet cheese case, near the tubs of fresh mozzarella and the French cheeses. Don't cut corners, since it's the main flavor in this dish.

Makes 4 servings.

INGREDIENTS
12 ounces dried spaghetti
8 tablespoons butter (1 stick)
**1½–2 tablespoons freshly ground black pepper, depending on
   how spicy you want the final dish**
1½ cups freshly grated, high-quality Parmesan or Pecorino Romano cheese
Optional: ½ cup Parmesan or Pecorino Romano

STEPS
1. Melt the butter in a nonstick skillet over medium heat. Add the pepper, stir well, and turn off the heat.

2. Cook the spaghetti according to the instructions on page 37. Before draining the pasta in step 6, reserve 2 cups of the cooking water from the pasta. After draining the pasta, return it to the pot.

3. Add 1½ cups of the cooking water to the nonstick pan with the butter and pepper. Stir to combine. Turn the heat back on to medium-high, and bring the water to a simmer.

4. Pour the water-and-butter mixture into the pot with the drained pasta. Using tongs, toss the pasta to coat it with the liquid. Add the grated cheese and use the tongs to toss the pasta until the cheese has melted and coated the noodles. If the pasta is too dry, add some of the unused reserved cooking water.

5. Serve with extra cheese, and pass the pepper grinder for people to add their own.

GOURMET HACK

Top with a fried egg, sliced chicken, or sautéed mushrooms.

Baking 101

Baking means cooking in an oven using dry heat. While you can bake all sorts of ingredients, from fish to breads, we'll focus on the really fun (and relatively simple) stuff in this section — things like cookies and muffins.

Tips

1. Different recipes will require different temperatures for baking. Be sure to read through your recipe first to see if it indicates cold or room-temperature ingredients.

2. When measuring, it's important to be precise. Think of baking as a science project! Recipes provide the right ratio of ingredients for a great end product. For dry ingredients, use measuring cups and spoons. Fill gently until heaping, and then level with the straight edge of a knife.

3. Cracking eggs can sometimes get tricky, and you don't want any shells in your treats. To avoid this, crack the egg into a small bowl before adding to your recipe.

4. Is your end result undercooked? Burnt? The problem could be your oven! Oven knobs rely on internal thermometers, so when you turn the dial to 350°F, it's using its internal measurement. Unfortunately, these thermometers can break. If you notice that your baked goods are consistently suffering, you can purchase an oven thermometer and follow the manufacturer's directions to adjust your oven temperature.

5. Similar to the above tip, ovens often have warmer and cooler spots. You can help offset the effect of these areas by rotating your baking sheet or pans halfway through your cooking time.

6. What's with those racks? Ovens have several rack settings to accommodate different recipe needs. Generally, the center rack is best for baking, and you will do great by keeping the rack there. (Still curious about all those rack slots? Loosely explained, you would want to lower your rack to promote browned bottoms, and raise your rack to promote browned tops.)

CHOCOLATE CHIP COOKIES

Makes about 24 cookies.

INGREDIENTS
½ cup (1 stick) salted butter at room temperature
½ cup granulated sugar
½ cup light brown sugar, packed firmly in the measuring cup
1 teaspoon vanilla extract
2 eggs
2¼ cups flour
1 teaspoon baking soda
¼ teaspoon salt
2 cups chocolate chips
Nonstick cooking spray

STEPS
1. Preheat your oven to 375°F. Spray a baking sheet with nonstick cooking spray.

2. Measure out your dry ingredients: flour, baking soda, and salt. Mix them together in a medium bowl.

3. In a large bowl, cream together the butter, granulated sugar, brown sugar, and vanilla with an electric mixer until combined. Add eggs one at a time, and beat well.

4. Add in the flour mixture in approximately four batches, mixing well each time until completely combined.

5. Stir in chocolate chips.

6. Drop a heaping tablespoon of dough onto the cookie sheet, leaving about 1 inch around each ball of dough to allow for spreading.

7. Bake for 8-10 minutes, until lightly browned. Repeat with the remaining dough, spraying with nonstick cooking spray between batches. Cool slightly before serving.

GOURMET HACK
Add ½ cup chopped walnuts in step 5.

TIME HACK
Make the cookie dough a day or two in advance! Just cover with plastic wrap and keep in the fridge. Then start the baking process with step 6. If the dough is too cold to scoop, just let it sit for a few minutes.

A Family Celebration Dinner

Delicious home-cooked meals are the perfect way to celebrate special occasions with your family and friends. To surprise them with your newfound cooking skills, throw a simple dinner party for graduation or as a birthday treat.

The Menu
Salad with balsamic vinaigrette
Cacio e pepe
Chocolate chip cookies

VARIETY HACK
Add olives, sliced tomatoes, or cucumbers to your salad.

GOURMET HACK
Use the chocolate chip cookies and a tub of vanilla ice cream to make ice cream sandwiches.

DORM ROOM DINING

When you first head off to college, the meal plan seems like the most amazing thing ever. You get to pick what you want from an extensive menu at EVERY SINGLE MEAL! You're no longer subject to the whim of a parent's or a picky sibling's weird taste. Want a cheeseburger? You've got it. Macaroni and cheese? At your fingertips.

So why learn about dorm-room cooking? Why bother to make your own meals when you have a cornucopia of cafeteria options to choose from? Here's why:

1. The novelty wears off pretty quickly. You'll find that much of the food is pretty mediocre, and you'll start falling into patterns where you eat the same thing over and over again. You'll want a change of pace from time to time.

2. You're in college and therefore keep really strange hours. The dining hall won't always be open, especially when you're starving at 3 a.m. while cramming for an exam.

3. Sometimes you just don't want to leave your dorm room. Maybe it's raining. Maybe you know your hot ex will be in the cafeteria and you just can't even deal with it. Maybe you have a date in your room and want to impress them.

4. Maybe you want to avoid the fabled "freshman fifteen," or you want to be conscious of what you eat. Cooking your own food allows you to control which ingredients you use.

Some simple planning — along with a basic arsenal of equipment and an airtight container with a few nonperishable ingredients — will cover you for all of these situations. Start by stockpiling extra napkins, straws, and plastic utensils. When you order takeout or delivery, save those salt and pepper packets, sauce packets, and the red pepper flakes that come with your meal. From there, you can add a few grocery store ingredients and some dining hall food to create dishes you won't believe came out of a dorm room!

Dorm Room Pantry

There are a few ingredients with long shelf lives that you can keep on hand to add a huge punch of flavor to almost any dish. The dorm-room pantry is all about adding your own flavors and stocking staples that allow you to create delicious food in the comfort of your dorm.

Before you shop for your food, have a chat with your roommate(s) to agree on a few rules. You'll want to be aware of any dietary restrictions, religious constraints, food allergies, and even sensitivity to certain food smells. (The worst way to make new friends? Burnt popcorn or canned tuna.)

HOT SAUCE

A drizzle of hot sauce can really turn a bland dish into something crave-worthy. Keep a bottle of your favorite kind on hand to add to soups and stews, drizzle over popcorn or a boring chicken breast, spice up a baked potato, or make hummus more interesting.

CURRY POWDER AND CURRY PASTE

Both are available in mild and spicy varieties. They are blends of spices and herbs that come together perfectly to capture the flavors of different countries. You can find Indian curry powder and Thai curry paste in most grocery stores, and Japanese curry tends toward the sweet and less spicy side. See the recipes for curry lime popcorn (page 74) and coconut curry ramen (page 59) to get inspired.

SOY SAUCE

An ingredient that adds a salty, savory flavor to any dish (not just sushi!). Try using a low-sodium option, as soy sauce can get quite salty. Start with only a splash and add more in small increments; soy sauce can take a dish from perfect to inedible pretty quickly. It's fantastic in salad dressings, soups, and sauces.

RAMEN NOODLES

Ramen is a college student's best friend. It's a quick, cheap, hot meal when you don't have the time, energy, or resources to do anything else. See pages 57–61 for healthier, tastier, and more nourishing ways to use your ramen noodles.

HOT CHOCOLATE

Envelopes of hot chocolate mix are great to satisfy your sweet tooth and warm you up on cold days. And they yield more than just a drink! Check out the recipe on page 71 to make a decadent mug brownie.

MICROWAVE POPCORN

Another college staple, microwave popcorn is the perfect snack (or occasional meal; just don't tell your mom). Try to keep some of the plain stuff and add your own toppings to turn it into a really flavorful treat.

Food Storage

Dorm-room meal prep requires some unique planning, including understanding how to store food. Since each school's dorms will likely have their own rules and regulations about equipment, let's start with the most basic task: keeping nonperishable food items on hand.

All of the steps in this section involve keeping your food items locked up where they aren't exposed to air. This is a great rule to keep in mind for food storage in general – and don't expect others to remember all the time. Alyssa's college had a huge mouse infestation, and she's still scarred. Leaving your food out in the open not only encourages animals (like mice and roaches) to seek you out for a midnight snack but also makes your food go bad sooner.

Keep a large clear plastic bin with a locking lid right in your room. The best size is a 30-quart container, which is large enough to handle tall bottles and full bags of chips but easily stashes into a corner. Make sure that you look for clear plastic, so that you can easily see which ingredients you have on hand. Latching handles that click into place to show the top is secure are an easy choice to ensure you don't start feeding any unwanted critters in your dorm space – no matter how much you and your roommate like animals.

In addition to your bin, keep a small stash of sealable plastic storage bags on hand. Bags take up almost no space and are great for all sorts of uses. Use them for storing leftovers that don't need to be refrigerated or standing in for that chip bag you tore open beyond repair. In fact, you probably can't go wrong putting items in these storage bags and then into your larger storage bin – you can never have too many extra layers of protection! Start with some gallon bags and quart bags. Don't forget to reuse clean bags if possible. Label your food with a permanent marker for any shared refrigerators.

If you find you have room for a few more items, consider some disposable plastic containers. You'll find them in grocery and drugstore aisles near the plastic wrap. Although they're meant to be disposable, you can actually use them several times before you throw them away. You only need to replace them when they've started to smell after washing or are no longer airtight. When your bins are full and can't hold anything more, these containers can easily hold and store snack items, like nuts and cereal from the cafeteria.

Food Safety

In addition to proper food storage, there are some things you need to do to ensure that you are taking care of your space and not eating spoiled food. These tasks seem small, but they can save you a lot of trouble.

DON'T IGNORE WEIRD FOOD SMELLS.

If you get a whiff of something nasty when you open your door, don't ignore it! Instead, do some investigating. You won't believe how easy it is to forget a banana and let it fall behind your desk. The thing is, it's not going to get any better unless you find the source of the smell and get rid of it. Cover your hands with trash bags and throw the item away immediately.

DON'T IGNORE SMALL BUGS EITHER.

If you found a weird food smell, chances are you may have also noticed small bugs floating around your space or ants creeping in corners. Those little flying bugs are likely fruit flies, and they come around when you've got food out in the open for them to eat. Of course, they especially like food that is starting to rot, because it smells sweet to them. Don't assume these bugs will just go away on their own. Investigate, find the source, and get rid of it.

TRY TO PUT DATES ON PERISHABLE FOODS.

It may be convenient to get "sick" when you have a big paper due, but it's never good to actually get sick. Keep a permanent marker handy, and label any food containers with their expiration dates before you put them in the refrigerator. You can even write the expiration date directly on eggshells! If you're not sure how long an item is safe, do a quick online search for guidelines. If that seems like too much work, use your nose. Bad food smells funky.

CLEAN OUT REFRIGERATORS REGULARLY.

If you're lucky enough to have your own fridge, just set a weekly calendar reminder on your phone or computer, so you don't forget to clean it out. Throw away anything that is past its expiration date. If you have any food that is still good to eat but you know you won't do so, ask a friend if they'd like it so that it doesn't just sit there and start to go bad. Clean up any spills.

TAKE OUT THE TRASH.

Yes, it's annoying and your roommate never does it. But keeping food out in the open is the best way to invite unwanted pets, and the trash can is the first place they turn up.

If you share a refrigerator with roommates, keep an eye on your food and everyone else's. It's so easy to forget what you put in there! Try to get everyone to agree on a cleaning schedule, and work together to prevent old food from taking up space. If the fridge gets nasty, you'll all stop using it, and it will just become a toxic-waste storage container.

Dorm Room Equipment

While each dorm situation is different, there is generally a shared space you will be able to use to cook your own meals or make a snack. Here's some of the most popular equipment to which you might have access, as well as some options you may be able to purchase and keep in your own room.

HOT PLATES

Hot plates are small appliances that generally resemble one of the heating elements you might find on an electric stovetop. Check to see if your campus allows these.

MICROWAVE OVENS

You've probably used these before! Microwaves are great and versatile appliances that are super useful for heating food and for cooking. Here are a few key tips worth mentioning:

Never put metal (or any item containing metal, including food takeout containers) into the microwave. It's a surefire way to start a blaze!

Keep your microwave clean! Set a paper towel on top of your dish to avoid splatters. If you find that you've made a mess, address it right away by wiping the interior down with a wet paper towel or sponge.

Microwave power is measured in watts. You will likely find that your dorm is equipped with lower-wattage models (700 to 900 watts). For our microwave recipes, we used a 700-watt microwave oven but offered a range for the cooking times. If you're using a microwave with a higher wattage, you'll want to set your cooking times on the shorter side. Online microwave-timing conversion charts are a good place to start for learning about cooking time differences.

MICROWAVE STEAMERS

Once you're sure you have microwave access, consider purchasing a plastic or silicone microwave steamer. To use, simply add water to the bottom of the steamer basket to quickly cook veggies, seafood, and even chicken! Not only does this make for fast meals, but the process of steaming your food is incredibly healthy because it doesn't involve extra oils or fats.

ELECTRIC KETTLES

Electric kettles are a great example of an appliance that looks simple but really offers you a lot of options. These kettles perform one task: boiling water quickly. Once your water is ready, you can use it to easily make tea, coffee, hot chocolate, instant soup, and oatmeal.

Stretching Your Meal Plan

Even if you decide not to eat in the dining hall, you can still use your meal plan to make simple dorm room food more delicious, healthier, and extra gourmet.

SALAD BAR

The salad bar is a gold mine for college students. You can stash some lettuce in your fridge for a healthy meal. Take some spinach and add it to your mushroom and cheese egg bowl (page 66). Keep veggies around and snack on them with some ranch dressing, or add them to pasta and soup. Take some of the shredded cheese home with you for eggs, grilled cheese, or nachos. Nuts are great for snacking or adding to a brownie in a mug (page 71). Most salad bars have oil and vinegar in separate containers, which you can take home in condiment cups and use in recipes. And, of course, it's always great to have condiments and dressings like ketchup, mustard, ranch dressing, and balsamic vinegar on hand.

BREAD

Use sandwich bread to make your own grilled cheese or toast. Grab a bagel or English muffin on Friday to save for a Saturday-morning (or afternoon) breakfast sandwich without setting foot outside. Pieces of baguette can be sliced into crostini (see page 130) for fancy snacks.

GRILLED OR ROASTED CHICKEN

Get an extra piece of roasted chicken and keep it in your fridge. You can shred it and add it to pasta, eggs, ramen, or other soups. Cubes of grilled chicken turn a salad into a full meal.

HARD-BOILED EGGS

These make for a terrific snack or breakfast, and they also add protein to a salad. They're a pretty fantastic addition to ramen too.

Better Salads

Bottled salad dressings are full of strange ingredients that keep the oil and vinegar from separating. Using the salad dressings you find at the salad bar can be even more mysterious than buying your own at the grocery store, because they're often poured into larger serving containers, obscuring ingredients and nutrition facts.

Since we've already shown you how easy it is to make your own dressings, continue using your pantry ingredients to make the dressings on page 17. In addition to those classic dressings, here are two more you can make using ingredients from your own pantry or the cafeteria.

SESAME SOY DRESSING

Makes 2 servings.

INGREDIENTS
1 tablespoon low-sodium soy sauce
1 tablespoon rice wine vinegar
1 tablespoon sesame oil
1 tablespoon extra virgin olive oil
1 clove garlic, minced, or ¼ teaspoon garlic powder
½ teaspoon sugar
½ teaspoon salt

LEMON MUSTARD VINAIGRETTE

Makes 2 servings.

INGREDIENTS
2 tablespoons extra virgin olive oil
1 tablespoon lemon juice
1 tablespoon red wine vinegar
1 tablespoon Dijon mustard
¼ teaspoon salt
¼ teaspoon pepper
Optional: 1 clove garlic, minced, or ¼ teaspoon garlic powder

STEPS FOR EACH
1. Combine all ingredients in an airtight container.

2. Shake for 15 seconds to emulsify.

3. Taste, and adjust salt and pepper as necessary.

Ramen Hacks

If there's one food that comes to mind when people think of college dining, it's instant ramen. Instant ramen is inexpensive and easy to make, and it can make you feel like you're getting one whole meal in a tiny packet.

Most of the following recipes assume that you have access to a hot plate, electric kettle, or stove. If you don't, use the liquid indicated in the recipe (water or broth) and follow the microwave instructions on the package. You'll also notice that many of these recipes use chicken or vegetable broth instead of the tiny foil flavoring packs that come with the noodles. These are packed with sodium and MSG (monosodium glutamate), but you can use your own ingredients to control the saltiness and add flavor. Boxed broth is inexpensive, doesn't need to be refrigerated until opened, is packed full of flavor, and can be pretty darn healthy. Keep it in your pantry bin. Once you've opened it, just label the container with your name and pop it in your fridge.

SPICY EGG DROP RAMEN

Makes 1 generous serving.

INGREDIENTS
1 cup chicken-flavored instant ramen noodles
2 cups water
1 egg
1 teaspoon your favorite chili sauce or hot sauce

STEPS
1. Heat the water to a boil in a microwave or electric kettle.

2. Fill the ramen cup as instructed and cover for 90 seconds.

3. Meanwhile, crack the egg into a small bowl, and scramble it well with a fork.

4. Slowly drizzle the egg into the cup of noodles, stirring with the fork to mix in the egg. Cover the cup again and let it sit for 3 minutes.

5. Stir in the hot sauce.

RAMEN WITH HAM, EGG, AND SPINACH

Makes 1 generous serving.

INGREDIENTS
1 package ramen noodles
2 cups chicken or vegetable stock
1 hard-boiled egg, shelled and sliced in half
2 slices deli ham, cut into ½-inch-thick slices
Handful of fresh spinach leaves
Optional: sliced green onions

STEPS
1. Pour the chicken stock into a medium saucepan and bring to a boil over high heat.

2. Add the ramen noodles and cook until al dente (about 5 minutes).

3. Place the spinach in the bottom of a large bowl. Pour the ramen noodles and chicken stock over the spinach and stir. Top with the egg and ham (and green onions, if using).

COCONUT CURRY RAMEN

Makes 1 generous serving.

INGREDIENTS
1 package ramen noodles
1½ cups chicken or vegetable stock
½ cup coconut milk or cream
1–1½ tablespoons red or green Thai curry paste
Optional: ½ cup shredded or cubed chicken

STEPS
1. Pour the chicken stock and coconut milk into a medium saucepan, and bring it to a boil over high heat. Add the curry paste and stir to dissolve and combine.

2. Add the ramen noodles and cook until al dente (about 5 minutes).

3. Pour the ramen noodles and liquid into a large bowl. Top with the chicken and enjoy.

Spice It Up

If you're feeling adventurous, you can try different chili pastes instead of hot sauce, such as Tunisian harissa, Korean gochujang, Japanese yuzu kosho, or sambal oelek from Southeast Asia.

BUDGET HACK

Use hard-boiled eggs and spinach from the dining hall salad bar.

RAMEN SALAD WITH CABBAGE AND CARROTS

Makes 1 generous serving.

INGREDIENTS
1 package ramen noodles
2 cups water
2 tablespoons sesame soy dressing (page 55)
½ cup shredded cabbage
¼ cup shredded carrots

BUDGET HACK
This dish is just as delicious the next day, served cold. Don't throw away your leftovers!

STEPS

1. Bring the water to a boil over high heat. Add the ramen noodles and cook until al dente (about 5 minutes). Drain the noodles in a colander and set them aside.

2. Return the pot to medium heat. Add the sesame soy dressing to the pot and then add the cabbage and carrots. Cook until the vegetables have softened slightly (about 3 minutes).

3. Add the noodles back to the pot and toss to combine.

RAMEN SALAD WITH PEANUT SAUCE AND EDAMAME

Makes 1 generous serving.

INGREDIENTS
1 package ramen noodles
2 cups water
2 tablespoons peanut sauce (can be found in the Asian section of grocery stores)
¼ cup shelled edamame (soybeans)
Optional: 1 tablespoon chopped peanuts, sliced green onions

HEARTY HACK
Add chicken or shrimp.

STEPS

1. Bring the water to a boil over high heat. Add the ramen noodles and cook until al dente (about 5 minutes). Drain the noodles in a colander and return them to the pot.

2. Add the peanut sauce to the pot and toss to combine. Place the sauced noodles on a plate or in a bowl.

3. Top with the shelled edamame (and peanuts and green onions, if using).

Microwave Recipes

You don't need access to a full kitchen to make something delicious. All you need is a microwave, some basic equipment, and a few ingredients. These recipes include some great ideas for meals, snacks, and desserts – we promise we won't judge if you want a brownie at 10 a.m.

MOZZARELLA IN MARINARA SAUCE

Serve this on crusty Italian bread or with garlic bread (below) for a delicious cheesy snack. Makes 4 servings.

INGREDIENTS
1 cup pizza sauce or marinara sauce
1 large ball fresh mozzarella cheese packed in liquid, about 5 grams

STEPS
1. Pour pizza sauce into a large mug or medium microwavable dish.

2. Pull the mozzarella out of the liquid and cut into quarters. Add it to the mug, and cover with the remaining pizza sauce.

3. Cover with a paper towel, and microwave on high for 90 seconds. Stir and cook 10 seconds at a time, until cheese is melted and stringy.

4. Scoop a spoonful of melty, cheesy sauce out of the bowl and spread onto the bread slices.

GARLIC BREAD

Makes 4 servings.

INGREDIENTS
2 tablespoons salted butter
¼ teaspoon garlic salt
Half a baguette or crusty Italian bread, cut into inch-thick slices

STEPS
1. Place the butter and garlic salt in a small microwavable bowl. Cover with a paper towel, and microwave on high heat for 30 seconds.

2. Use a spoon to drizzle the garlic butter over the slices of bread.

SPICY EDAMAME

Makes 1 serving.

INGREDIENTS
1 ½ teaspoons soy sauce
½ teaspoon garlic powder
½ teaspoon sesame oil
½–1 teaspoon chili sauce or hot sauce
1 cup of cooked, shell-on edamame

STEPS
1. Combine the soy sauce, garlic powder, sesame oil, and chili sauce in a medium bowl. Stir well to combine.

2. Add the edamame to the bowl, and toss to combine.

MUSHROOM AND CHEESE EGG BOWL

Makes 1 serving.

INGREDIENTS
2 eggs
1 teaspoon milk
½ teaspoon salt
⅛ teaspoon pepper
½ tablespoon butter, cut into small cubes
2 mushrooms, cut into ¼-inch slices
**Half of a string cheese, shredded
(about 1 ounce shredded cheese)**

STEPS

1. Crack the eggs into a mug or bowl. Add the milk, salt, and pepper. Beat with a fork to break the yolks and combine the ingredients.

2. Add the butter, mushrooms, and cheese.

3. Cover with a paper towel, and microwave on high heat for 1 minute. Check to see if the eggs have set. If not, repeat for 10 seconds at a time until they're cooked through. Don't overcook them! They'll get rubbery and smell funky.

GOURMET AND BUDGET HACKS

Raid your cafeteria's salad bar for add-ins! Stir in green onions, spinach, diced tomatoes, or bacon crumbles in step 2.

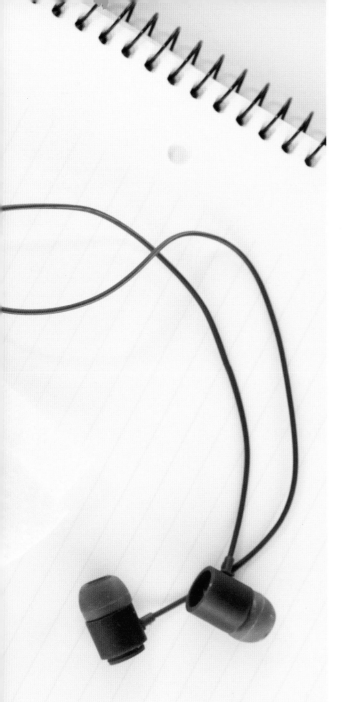

BREAKFAST BREAD PUDDING

Makes 1 serving.

INGREDIENTS
½ tablespoon butter
3 tablespoons milk
1 egg
¼ teaspoon cinnamon
½ teaspoon vanilla
1½ tablespoons sugar
2 slices of bread, cut or torn into
   ¾-inch cubes
Optional for serving: maple syrup

STEPS
1. Place the butter in a large mug or medium microwavable bowl. Microwave on high for 10–20 seconds, until melted. Add the milk and stir with a fork.

2. Crack the egg into the butter mixture. Add the cinnamon, vanilla, and sugar. Beat well with the fork. Add the bread cubes, and mix well to coat the bread.

3. Microwave uncovered for 90 seconds, and check to see if the egg is still runny. Microwave for 10 seconds at a time, until the egg has set.

4. Drizzle with maple syrup, if using.

GOURMET AND BUDGET HACKS

Stir in raisins, chopped nuts, or chocolate chips from your dining hall's sundae bar or oatmeal station. Use day-old pastries such as brioche or croissants for the bread.

SIMPLE BROWNIE

Makes 1 serving.

INGREDIENTS
1 tablespoon butter
2 tablespoons vegetable oil
2 tablespoons milk
2 packets hot chocolate mix (about 5 tablespoons)
4 tablespoons flour

STEPS
1. Place the butter in a large mug or medium microwavable bowl. Microwave on high for 15–30 seconds, until melted. Add the milk and oil, and stir with a fork.

2. Add the chocolate mix and flour to the mug, and blend thoroughly with a fork until completely combined.

3. Cover with a paper towel and microwave on high for 60 seconds. Check for doneness and cook for 10 seconds at a time, until the brownie has puffed up and is no longer wobbly.

GOURMET HACKS
Stir chopped nuts or chocolate chips into the batter in step 2. Top with a scoop of ice cream.

CHOCOLATE-DIPPED PRETZELS AND CHIPS

Makes 2 servings.

INGREDIENTS
1 small bag pretzels
1 small bag potato chips (try kettle chips)
½ cup or 3 ounces of your favorite chocolate (about 2 candy bars)

STEPS
1. Break the chocolate into small pieces and place in a medium microwavable bowl. Microwave on high for 20 seconds. Stir with a spoon and continue to microwave in 10-second intervals, stirring until the chocolate has melted. This should take 45–60 seconds.

2. Dip the pretzels and the potato chips in the chocolate, and set on a sheet of wax paper to cool.

3. Enjoy once the chocolate has cooled. To speed up the process, you can place the pretzels or chips in the refrigerator.

GOURMET AND FUN HACKS
Sprinkle with flaky sea salt or chopped nuts. Use cinnamon and sugar pretzels or flavored potato chips. Shake colored sprinkles over the chocolate after dipping the pretzels.

Gourmet Popcorn Hacks

Microwave popcorn is a college student's best friend for late-night snacks, when the cafeterias are closed and you're pulling an all-nighter. Step up your popcorn game with these gourmet flavors.

Microwave on high until the popcorn kernels wait more than 3 seconds between pops. Remove from the microwave, pour into a large bowl, and add your toppings. Toss to combine.

Start experimenting with the recipes and hacks on the next pages. If you're looking to take your popcorn to the next level, try making your own microwave popcorn. Find dried kernels on the cheap in the bulk bins of your grocery store, or look for a large jar by the microwavable popcorn. Place ¼ cup of kernels into a brown paper lunch bag, fold over the top inch of the bag and use *only* one staple to close the bag. Microwave as usual.

OLIVE OIL AND PARMESAN POPCORN

Use microwave popcorn with no flavors added. The Parmesan cheese should be salty enough, and the olive oil will replace the butter.

Makes 1 bag.

INGREDIENTS
1 bag popped popcorn
2 tablespoons extra virgin olive oil
¼ cup grated Parmesan cheese

STEPS

1. Empty the popcorn into a large bowl.

2. Drizzle olive oil over popcorn and toss to coat.

3. Sprinkle Parmesan cheese over the popcorn and toss to coat.

GOURMET HACK

Add 1 teaspoon of freshly cracked black pepper.

CURRY LIME POPCORN

Makes 1 bag.

INGREDIENTS
1 bag popped popcorn, buttered or unflavored
1 lime
1–1½ tablespoons curry powder

STEPS

1. Empty the popcorn into a large bowl.

2. Cut the lime in half, and squeeze the juice from one of the halves over the popcorn. Toss to coat. Add 1 tablespoon of the curry powder and toss again to distribute the curry powder.

3. Taste the popcorn. If you'd like more flavor, you can add more lime or curry.

CHOCOLATE AND PEANUT POPCORN

Makes 1 bag.

INGREDIENTS
1 bag popped popcorn, buttered or unflavored
½ cup or 3 ounces your favorite chocolate (about 2 candy bars)
½ cup roasted and salted peanuts

STEPS
1. Empty the popcorn into a large bowl.

2. Break the chocolate into small pieces and place in a medium microwavable bowl. Microwave on high heat for 20 seconds. Stir with a spoon and continue to microwave in 10-second intervals, stirring until the chocolate has melted. This should take 45–60 seconds.

3. Drizzle half of the chocolate over the popcorn, and toss to mix. Add half of the nuts and toss again. Repeat with the remaining chocolate and nuts.

4. For melty chocolate, you can eat immediately. For harder chocolate, wait about an hour and break into chunks. You can eat it like a popcorn ball. Eat within a few hours of making to avoid stale popcorn.

FUN HACK
Add a few tablespoons of colored sprinkles at the end, and toss to coat.

Dorm Room Movie Night

Invite a few close friends to your room for a movie night, or bring snacks to the common area or lounge to make new friends on your floor. Price of admission? Everyone brings their own mug to make their brownie!

The Menu

Curry lime popcorn
Olive oil and Parmesan popcorn
Chocolate and peanut popcorn
Chocolate-dipped pretzels and chips
Simple brownie

MOVIE-NIGHT HACK

Everyone brings a different topping and their own bag of plain microwave popcorn. Share your favorite combinations and try new ones.

EXTRA TOPPING IDEAS

Chocolate-covered caramels

Mini peanut-butter cups

Soy sauce

Hot sauce

Sesame oil

Ranch seasoning

FIRST APARTMENT DINING

Once you've moved into a larger kitchen with roommates, you'll have so much more pantry space! You also get to enjoy the kitchen space with your friends, cooking together and sharing meals. This is super fun, and we both have great memories of "family" dinners and potlucks.

But there are precautions you'll need to take to make it a great and easy experience for all the roommates involved. Because it's time for some real talk – these were actual roommate experiences we both had (we won't name names):

• The roommate who never did dishes, so they piled up in the sink and attracted bugs.

• The roommate who stole ingredients, but only the good, fancy ones.

• The roommate who put mostly smelly things in the trash but never emptied it.

You get the picture.

This section provides plenty of guidelines for a peaceful shared-kitchen experience to avoid the issues above. We also included information about stretching leftovers and pantry ingredients into multiple meals. Best of all, the recipes are classics that are great for sharing.

Kitchen Etiquette

(So you don't get kicked out or require an intervention!) Sharing a kitchen with roommates can sometimes be challenging. Here are some guidelines to maintain a harmonious living environment:

• Clean up after yourself the day you make a mess. Don't leave your dishes in the sink overnight or leave crumbs on the counter. Overnight can quickly turn into two days, then a week, then your roommates not speaking to you.

• Clean out the refrigerator periodically. Maybe you forgot that you brought home leftover salmon from the restaurant, but in a few weeks you'll wonder what smells so awful.

• Chip in and share. If you used most of the flour to make a batch of cookies, buy more the next time you go to the store. If one of your roommates seems to buy all of the groceries all the time, throw them some money for eggs and milk from time to time.

• If you run into issues, you may find it necessary to label your groceries. If you can't live without ranch dressing, put your name on the bottle and explain to your roommates that you want to make sure you never run out. Or if you spent a small fortune on a really good bottle of olive oil, request that they ask you before using it (or better yet, just tell them it's off limits). Don't assume that they won't use it just because they didn't buy it.

• Use sealed containers. Store leftovers in plastic containers to reduce food smells. Tightly seal condiments and jars. Get airtight containers for flour and sugar even if you just use plastic bags. Critters in the kitchen are never good.

• This may seem like common sense, and some of it may even seem a bit extreme, but more than one friendship has gone sour because of disagreements over groceries and kitchen messes!

First Apartment Pantry

Setting up a kitchen requires a bit of a financial investment up front, but most pantry staples will last for quite a while. Refer to these buying tips to help you understand how to select these ingredients.

EXTRA VIRGIN OLIVE OIL
High-quality extra virgin olive oil is absolutely essential! Look for oil with a press date on the label, as much supermarket oil can be old and even rancid. Ideally, you would consume olive oil within a year of its press date. Buy a small bottle so it doesn't go bad before you can use it.

COOKING OIL (SUCH AS CANOLA OR SAFFLOWER)
Cooks tend to grab olive oil first when cooking, but it is not as well suited to high temperatures, and it has a distinct flavor that isn't necessarily desirable in every dish or every type of cuisine. A neutral oil, such as canola or safflower, holds up to high heat and has very little flavor. You'll need a large bottle if you're going to deep fry with the oil, but a smaller bottle will work for most recipes.

NONSTICK COOKING SPRAY
Although there are many options for nonstick cooking spray, a neutral and flavorless one is the most versatile option. You use very little in recipes, so one container will last a long time.

ALL-PURPOSE FLOUR

There are many different types of flour. All-purpose flour is the most versatile option, so it's best to stock a 5-pound bag of it and buy other types of flour (bread flour, cake flour, buckwheat flour) when a recipe calls for them specifically.

SUGAR (GRANULATED, LIGHT BROWN, AND CONFECTIONER'S)

It is useful to keep both a 2-pound bag of granulated sugar and a 1-pound bag of light brown sugar in your pantry. Dark brown sugar is also useful, but is generally not used as often as light brown. You can stock confectioner's sugar (aka powdered sugar or icing sugar) if you intend to bake often, as it's vital for frostings and glazes.

LOW-SODIUM CHICKEN STOCK

Chicken stock can be the base for soups and stews, and it adds a hint of meaty flavor to many dishes. Keep a few cans or boxes of low-sodium stock on hand, as you can always add salt to a dish but can't take it away! When cooking, it's best to start with the lowest level of salt possible and build from there. Just be sure to refrigerate after opening.

CANNED TOMATOES

While canned tomatoes are not a suitable substitute for fresh tomatoes in most recipes, they have many uses of their own. Start by keeping a few cans of whole Roma tomatoes or diced tomatoes. The unseasoned varieties are most versatile.

PASTA

Dried pasta can turn into a quick and easy meal and lasts for years when stored in an airtight container. If you have a package of spaghetti or penne, you'll always have a homemade dinner option.

WHITE OR BROWN RICE

Rice becomes a hearty and healthy meal when topped with vegetables, meats, or sauces. White rice cooks faster and is a blank canvas for other flavors, while brown rice is nuttier, firmer, and more nutritious. Keep a bag of rice on hand to throw together a weeknight meal.

VINEGAR (BALSAMIC, RED, OR WHITE WINE)

Vinegar has varying degrees of acidity and is perfect in salad dressings, sauces, and marinades. Balsamic vinegar is sweeter and has a lower level of acidity, while red or white wine vinegars are more bracing and have higher acidity levels. Buy small to medium-sized bottles, because a little bit goes a long way. Vinegar has an indefinite shelf life.

DIJON MUSTARD

Dijon is more versatile than the standard American ballpark mustard. It's less bracing and adds subtle flavor to fried or roasted chicken, salad dressings, and marinades. It's also perfect for sandwiches, hot dogs, sausages, and pretzels.

PEANUT BUTTER

Peanut butter makes amazing sandwiches and it's great on toast, but it's also used in sauces in many Asian countries. You can use it in many baking recipes as well. Keep a jar of crunchy or creamy peanut butter (depending on your preference) on hand.

YELLOW OR WHITE ONIONS

Onions are an important part of many recipes, so it's a good idea to have a few on hand. They can add a base of flavor to dishes, or they can be featured on their own when caramelized or grilled.

POTATOES

Potatoes are filling and versatile. You can cook them in many ways, such as roasting, mashing, or frying. They're great for breakfast, lunch, or dinner. If you keep a bag of Yukon gold potatoes in your pantry, you'll never go hungry!

GARLIC

A head of garlic contains about ten cloves, so you usually only need to keep one bulb on hand. Use it sparingly, unless the recipe specifically calls for large quantities – the taste of garlic is strong and can easily overwhelm a dish (and your palate!).

BUTTER

There are many options for butter in the supermarket. You don't need to keep every kind on hand, and we suggest keeping a few sticks of salted butter in your refrigerator. It's useful for most cooking purposes. Unsalted butter is better for baking, and spread butter is best for your morning toast.

EGGS

Eggs are arguably the most important ingredient in the kitchen, used in both baking and savory dishes. You can scramble, fry, boil, or poach them. They help batter stay on fried foods, enrich pasta dishes, and define breakfast. If you're approaching the expiration date on a carton of eggs, hard-boil them for a portable breakfast or to turn into egg salad. Buy half a dozen or a dozen eggs at a time, depending on your household size and how often you cook.

MILK

Milk is a nutritious ingredient for breakfast and baking. Keep a quart or gallon of 2 percent or whole milk in your refrigerator, based on how much cereal you eat.

LEMONS AND LIMES

Keep lemons or limes on hand to make vinaigrettes (see page 17), marinades, or simply to squeeze over dishes to add a hint of brightness. If you need to use them up, add a slice to your water for a boost of vitamin C.

JAM, MARMALADE, OR PRESERVES

If you have bread and jam, you'll always have a delicious breakfast or snack. Keep a jar of your favorite flavor in the refrigerator.

Helpful Hacks

Here are a few ideas to help take your pantry to the next level, by having ingredients on hand to hack your own recipes.

CANNED BEANS

Beans are a filling, healthy source of protein. You can add them to soups, pastas, salads, and chilis. Buy whatever kinds you like best, but garbanzo beans, white beans, and black beans are great starting points. There are seasoned ones out there, but you can get unseasoned ones and add your own spices and salt.

PASTA AND PIZZA SAUCE

A can or jar of your favorite pasta sauce is perfect for quick weeknight spaghetti meals or as pizza sauce. You can also stock pizza sauce, but your favorite tomato-based spaghetti sauce will work just as well. Store opened jars in the refrigerator, and don't be afraid to doctor the sauce to your own liking. Add more Italian seasoning, some fresh basil, a handful of Parmesan cheese, or some red pepper flakes.

HONEY

A natural sweetener with a distinct flavor, honey is amazing on Greek yogurt with granola, drizzled over apples or toast, and stirred into tea. Honey is also an ingredient in many baking recipes and savory dishes.

APPLES

You can always pick up a whole apple for a fantastic portable snack, or you can slice apples and add your favorite nut butter or cheese. They add sweet crunch to salads, can be cooked down as an ice cream topping, and make a perfect pie filling.

FROZEN CORN

Flash-frozen corn maintains the sweetness and texture of fresh corn better than canned. Stock a bag in your freezer to add color, texture, and sweetness to soups, stews, chilis, and fried rice.

FROZEN FRUIT

Frozen fruit can easily be added to cake, muffin, or scone recipes. Turn it into a sauce (page 119) for ice cream, yogurt, cakes, and pancakes. Add some to a smoothie. Berry mixes are probably the most versatile.

ICE CREAM

Vanilla ice cream is delicious on its own or dressed up with sauces. It's the perfect accompaniment to pies and cakes as well, making it a dessert essential, and it can even be used in milkshakes. Keep a pint in the freezer so you'll always have a quick dessert option.

The Spice Rack

KOSHER SEA SALT

Kosher sea salt is the culinary standard in kitchens. Assume that a recipe calls for this type of salt unless otherwise specified. It has large soft crystals that easily dissolve into food. If you need to use table salt, use half as much as the recipe indicates, since the grains are smaller and measure more densely. Start with a 1-pound box until you have a better idea of how often you cook and how much salt you use.

PEPPER

Pepper begins to lose its kick as soon as you crack it, so pre-ground pepper has relatively little flavor. Invest in a pepper grinder that you can refill, or you can buy disposable pepper grinders with whole peppercorns in the spice section of most grocery stores.

ONION POWDER AND GARLIC POWDER

Onion and garlic powders are full of concentrated flavor. A little goes a long way in adding seasoning to dishes, especially when you don't want pieces of onion or garlic in the end result. They are perfect for adding extra flavor to a dish near the end of cooking. Keep one small container of each.

ONION SALT AND GARLIC SALT

Onion and garlic salts serve the same purpose as onion and garlic powders, but they also add a bit of salty flavor to the dish. They're useful as well but are less versatile because you can add onion or garlic powder and salt separately to achieve the same result. If you only have the room or the budget for one, try onion and garlic powders.

ITALIAN SEASONING

Stock a small container, as Italian seasoning starts to lose flavor after about a year. It pairs naturally with anything tomato based and is an easy way to add flavor to pasta sauces and pizza.

VANILLA EXTRACT

Most recipes only call for 1-2 teaspoons, so start with a small bottle in your spice rack. Imitation vanilla is available as well, although real vanilla extract can have a better flavor.

GROUND CINNAMON

Ground cinnamon is a baking essential. It's used in pie, cake, and cookie recipes, and you can sprinkle it sparingly over finished baked goods for a spicy, aromatic finish. It starts to lose its punch after about six months, so you only need a small jar.

BAKING SODA AND BAKING POWDER

Keep small containers, as you only need minimal quantities of these ingredients for most recipes, and they expire after about one year.

Keep It Fresh

There are many useful dried herbs and spices that can add lots of flavor to dishes. Try to avoid purchasing a set of spices from big-box retailers. The product tends to be older than what you find in supermarkets, and most herbs and spices start to lose flavor after about six months. Buy the essentials listed in this book and add others to your pantry as you need them in recipes. It's helpful to use a permanent marker to record the date you opened the packaging, so you know when it's time to replace older herbs and spices.

First Apartment Equipment

Some of these items are incredibly easy to find at dollar stores, thrift stores, or garage sales! Kitchen tools with blades as well as knives, pots, and pans should be purchased new to ensure best quality. Discount department stores are a great resource for these items.

KITCHEN TOWELS
Look for towels that are soft and absorbent, without too many design elements (like embroidery) that can extend drying time. Thinner towels are a plus since they will dry quickly.

SILVERWARE, PLATES, AND BOWLS
Look for three-piece sets, which include dinner forks, spoons, and knives. To be economical, avoid sets that come with extras like soup spoons or salad forks that aren't necessary. Plates and bowls are best purchased in durable materials, such as tempered glass, sturdy ceramic, or melamine. A set of four will be sufficient, unless you are having many guests over.

GLASSES AND MUGS
As with servingware, four solid glass tumblers and four ceramic mugs will suit your needs. When selecting these, keep your storage space in mind so you don't purchase something too large.

CHEF'S KNIFE
Start with an 8-inch chef's knife. Look for a knife with some weight to it, one that feels solid and comfortable in your hand. Bonus points if you can find one where the blade extends through the handle.

PARING KNIFE
No need to buy a set of these – one sharp paring knife will be plenty.

CAN OPENER
Electric openers are simple but take up unnecessary space in the kitchen. Smooth-edge openers tend to be temperamental, so try a standard top-cut style.

CUTTING BOARDS
Cutting boards come in many materials: plastic, wood, and tempered glass. Bamboo cutting boards are our first pick, since they will help you keep the edges of your knives sharp. If you do invest in a wooden board, don't soak it or put it in the dishwasher. Wash right away and dry thoroughly after use. If you're looking to save space, opt for a lightweight plastic version.

VEGETABLE PEELER
Vegetable peelers come in several varieties. Look for peelers with swivel heads and easy-grip handles.

GARLIC PRESS
Look for a press made of stainless steel, since it won't hold any odors and is easy to clean. Hand wash right after using.

CHEESE GRATER
A box grater is ideal for grating ingredients such as vegetables and cheese on its four different grating surfaces. If you are tight on space, look for a handheld grater with medium-sized holes.

SPATULAS
Rubber or silicone spatulas are excellent for turning foods, stirring, or icing baked items – and are the only utensils to use on nonstick surfaces. A slotted fish spatula is a thin metal option that is lightweight and makes draining grease very easy. You will likely want one of each style.

WHISK
A simple tool you'll use more than you realize, whisks are relatively easy to buy, due to the lack of variety in their design. Find a medium-sized tool, about 8–10 inches long, with a thick handle.

WOODEN SPOONS

A kitchen essential, wooden spoons can last for a very long time. Look for a sturdy spoon with a substantial handle. If you have extra space, also purchase a slotted version for draining and a version with squared corners for scraping the corners of pans. Tip: Letting your wooden spoon soak in water will ruin it. Wash right away and dry thoroughly after use.

TONGS

Great for pan-frying and roasting, tongs are indispensable when working with very hot foods. Silicone tips are great for nonstick surfaces, since they won't damage the finish, but tongs also come in metal and wood options. Prioritize gripped handles with sturdy tips.

10-INCH NONSTICK PAN

Nonstick pans allow you to experiment with cooking techniques without having to worry about food sticking to the pan. Look for a sturdy pan (preferably lidded) with some weight to it. Ceramic options cook evenly, are easy to clean, and last longer than coated pans.

MEDIUM TO LARGE STOCKPOT

A 6-quart nonstick stockpot is the perfect size for cooking, whether for one or many. Look for an option that comes with a glass lid, which will allow you to check on your food without disrupting the cooking process.

LARGE BOWLS

Mixing bowls come in several sizes. Look for medium to large bowls instead of smaller bowls that make it harder to mix ingredients. The best choice is to purchase bowls that serve several functions, such as lidded stainless steel bowls that nest for easy storage and allow for stirring, serving, and storing foods.

MUFFIN PAN

One 12-cup aluminum muffin pan is sufficient.

COLANDER

Look for a noncollapsible version with medium-sized holes and a sturdy base, in plastic or silicone. There is no need to buy a tiny colander for small foods like berries – one medium colander will suit all your needs.

MEASURING CUPS AND SPOONS

These items are easy to find and available in a variety of materials. Keep it simple and purchase lightweight plastic options with measurements that are large and easy to read.

BAKING SHEETS

Rimmed baking sheets in lightweight aluminum are your best bet. While you can get away with only one sheet, buying two is best, so that you can use one for baking and one for roasting at high heat.

CASSEROLE DISH

A casserole dish is a great choice for cooking, transporting, and serving food. Start with a lidded glass 2-quart pan with handles, making it easy to remove from the oven when hot.

ALUMINUM FOIL AND PLASTIC WRAP

It's important to have one roll of each of these kitchen basics on hand. Aluminum foil is used more often in the cooking process, while plastic wrap is useful for food storage.

As you gain more space in your kitchen, the equipment gets better and better. At this point in your cooking adventures, you've probably started to identify your favorite types of food to eat and cook. With so many choices available, plan to invest in equipment that will make it easier for you to make your favorites. Here are some next-step tools to consider.

CAST-IRON PAN

Great for cooking on the stovetop or in the oven, this versatile pan requires less oil, is easy to clean, and is an inexpensive choice. Cooks swear by cast iron, and many have been cooking in the same pan for years. While these pans can be a little tricky to maintain (there are varying opinions on care – search online to learn more), they produce even heat distribution and wonderful cooking results. Start with a 10-inch cast-iron pan and follow the instructions that accompany it for seasoning and care.

2-QUART SAUCEPAN (SMALL POT)

Sure, you can make a sauce in a larger pot. But if you find that you're often cooking smaller quantities that tend to burn, buy this smaller pot. It is also a great size for reheating soups and leftovers, and it's easier to clean than its larger counterparts.

BLENDER

Blenders are useful for all kinds of cooking, from easy milkshakes to flavorful pureed soups. Look for a blender with a wide base that won't topple easily, and spring for the most powerful motor you can comfortably afford.

MIXER

A hand mixer works fine for the casual cook in most circumstances, and you may not need to splurge on a stand mixer. But if you like baking, it's a worthwhile investment. Buy a mixer with a bowl that locks in and a strong motor. If you're turning into a serious cook, invest in a model that is compatible with accessories, such as a pasta machine and ice cream maker.

SLOW COOKER/CROCKPOT

Slow cookers are a worthwhile investment for a busy person who loves to cook. They excel at easily cooking tender meat meals and at making soups and stews in a few set-it-and-forget-it steps. They can range from very affordable to incredibly expensive, so start with an inexpensive model and upgrade if you find yourself using it often. We don't include any recipes in this book that use them because there are countless cookbooks devoted to slow cookers, with recipes ranging from breakfast to dessert.

LIQUID MEASURING CUP

Sure, you can totally use your dry measuring cups to measure out liquid. But now that you have a bit more space, invest in a liquid measuring cup. Dry measuring cups are filled with dry ingredients, then leveled off with a knife. When you use the same cups to measure liquid, it's hard to fill it up exactly to the edge without spilling over, which means you get a slightly inaccurate measurement. A simple liquid measuring cup will improve your baking results and keep your counters nice and clean.

Intermediate Techniques and Recipes

You seriously won't believe how easy it is to make your own granola, biscuits, chicken, and more – and as soon as you learn how, you'll never want to stop.

GRANOLA

This recipe teaches you to make basic granola; then you can add all the dried fruits, nuts, and other tasty ingredients you can handle.

Makes 5 servings.

INGREDIENTS
2 cups old-fashioned oats
2 tablespoons honey
¼ cup light brown sugar
¼ cup vegetable, canola, or coconut oil
½ teaspoon kosher sea salt
½ teaspoon cinnamon
Nonstick cooking spray

STEPS

1. Preheat oven to 300°F. Spray a light layer of nonstick cooking spray over the cookie sheet.

2. Combine all of the ingredients in a medium bowl. Stir well to combine.

3. Spread the granola over the cookie sheet in an even layer.

4. Bake for 10 minutes. Stir the oats and break up any big clumps. Bake for 10 more minutes, stirring again. Bake for 5 minutes at a time, until the oats turn light golden brown. (They'll continue to cook slightly after you pull them out of the oven, so they'll still get darker.) Keep a close eye on them – they can go from toasted to burned very quickly!

5. Remove from oven and allow to cool completely. Store in an airtight container for up to a week.

GOURMET HACKS

Mix-ins for step 2
1 teaspoon vanilla extract, 1 teaspoon nutmeg or pumpkin pie spice, or substitute agave nectar or maple syrup for the honey

Add-ins for step 4
When you have about 10 minutes of cook time left, add ¼ cup of raw chopped nuts, hemp seeds, pepitas, sunflower seeds, or shredded coconut.

Delicious Extras
Once removed from the oven and cooled for 5 minutes, your granola is ready for ½ cup of these goodies: chocolate chips, chopped dried fruit, freeze-dried fruit, or dried coconut chips.

More Toast

Something magical happens when you put cinnamon and sugar under a broiler. Add warm, crisp bread to the equation, and you have a really easy and delicious breakfast or snack. It all starts with the cinnamon-and-sugar ratio.

CINNAMON SUGAR

INGREDIENTS
¼ cup granulated sugar
1 tablespoon cinnamon

STEPS

1. Combine the sugar and cinnamon in a small sealable bag or airtight container.

2. Seal and shake to combine.

GOURMET HACK

Add 1 tablespoon of cocoa powder to the mixture for a Mexican-chocolate-inspired version, or use pumpkin pie spice instead of cinnamon.

CINNAMON SUGAR TOAST

Makes 4 servings.

INGREDIENTS
4 pieces your favorite sliced bread
4 tablespoons butter
4 tablespoons cinnamon sugar (above)

HEALTHY HACK

Replace the butter with coconut oil.

STEPS

1. Preheat oven to 350°F.

2. Toast four slices of bread until golden brown.

3. Spread each slice of toasted bread thickly with about 1 tablespoon of butter.

4. Sprinkle about 1 tablespoon of cinnamon sugar onto each slice of buttered toast.

5. Arrange toast on a baking sheet and place in oven for 2–3 minutes, just long enough to crisp the cinnamon sugar on top of the toast.

APPLE PEANUT BUTTER TOAST

Throw apples and peanut butter into the mix, and you end up with a treat that could pass for either breakfast or dessert!

Makes 4 servings.

INGREDIENTS
4 slices your favorite bread
Peanut butter
1 apple, cored
About 2 tablespoons cinnamon sugar (page 92)

STEPS
1. Lightly toast the bread.

2. Set the oven rack to the top position, and heat your oven's broiler on high.

3. Cut your apple into ⅛-inch slices.

4. Spread a ¼-inch-thick layer of peanut butter on one side of the toast slices. Place on the cutting board and cover the peanut butter with a layer of apples, with the edges of the apples slightly overlapping. Sprinkle each piece with a light dusting of cinnamon sugar, about ¼–½ tablespoon per piece.

5. Move to the baking sheet and place under the broiler for 2–3 minutes, until the apples are soft and the sugar begins to bubble and caramelize.

GOURMET HACK

Try flavored peanut butter or other nut butters, such as almond or cashew. Substitute ripe pears for the apples.

The Bread

The bread aisle can be pretty overwhelming. It runs the gamut from pretty generic and neutral bread to healthy bread packed with nuts and seeds to sweet bread with cinnamon or raisins. It's really a matter of personal taste, so if you want a completely blank slate, then go ahead and reach for that fluffy white bread. If you are looking to eat healthier, try whole wheat or seven-grain bread. Just check the labels and try to avoid anything with too many additives or too much sugar. You'd be surprised how many ingredients that you can't even pronounce are on some bread labels!

Intermediate Baking

When most people hear the term *baking*, they imagine piles of desserts. But of course you can also bake savory items like breads and biscuits. These biscuits are easy to make, don't require any rolling or biscuit cutters, and are a total crowd pleaser.

DROP BISCUITS

Makes 8-10 biscuits.

INGREDIENTS
2 cups all-purpose flour
2 teaspoons baking powder
½ teaspoon baking soda
1 teaspoon sugar
¾ teaspoon salt
1 cup buttermilk
8 tablespoons salted butter, melted and slightly cooled
2 tablespoons melted butter (for brushing at the end)

STEPS

1. Preheat oven to 475°F and place the baking rack in the top ⅓ of the oven. Line a rimmed baking sheet with parchment paper.

2. Whisk dry ingredients together in a large bowl.

3. Stir buttermilk and 8 tablespoons of melted butter together in a small bowl. Use a rubber spatula (for easiest cleanup) to gently stir the buttermilk mixture into the flour mixture. Combine until the ingredients are just mixed together and you can't see any more dry flour. Don't overmix, or your biscuits will get tough.

4. Use a ¼ cup measuring cup to scoop out the dough and drop onto the prepared baking sheet. Space each biscuit about 1½ inches apart. You should get 8-10 biscuits, depending on how generous your scoops are.

5. Bake until the tops of the biscuits are just barely golden brown and slightly crisp, 12-14 minutes. Remove from the oven, brush with additional melted butter. Serve warm. Reheat leftover biscuits in a 350°F oven for about 5 minutes.

GOURMET HACK

Add ¼ cup of shredded cheddar cheese or cooked bacon to step 4.

SPICY HACK

Add ½ tablespoon of your favorite chili powder, paprika, or hot sauce to step 2.

Buttermilk

Buttermilk is a tangy dairy ingredient that is often called for in baking, but you might not have it on hand. The good news is you can easily create a substitute using your pantry ingredients! Simply add 1 tablespoon of white vinegar or lemon juice into the bottom of a liquid measuring cup. Then fill the cup up to the "1 cup" line with milk. Let it stand for 5 minutes, then stir with a spoon, and measure out as much as you need for your recipe.

How to Sauté

SAUTÉ: A fast and easy cooking method involving a bit of oil and chopped ingredients over medium-high to high heat.

TIPS:

• Cut ingredients into small, similarly sized pieces. This will help ensure that the food cooks at the same rate.

• Start with a hot pan. If you are using a nonstick pan, avoid heating for too long because it can scorch and ruin the coating—30 seconds max! Once the pan is hot, heat your oil for about 10-15 seconds.

• Don't use too many ingredients for your pan size. This is called *overcrowding* and can prevent your food from cooking properly.

GROUND BEEF AND POTATO TACOS

Makes 12 tacos.

INGREDIENTS
½ large onion, chopped
2 tablespoons olive oil
1 pound ground beef
1 clove of garlic, chopped or crushed
½ teaspoon kosher sea salt
¼ teaspoon freshly ground black pepper
3 medium potatoes (preferably Yukon Gold potatoes), scrubbed and cubed
1 8-ounce can of tomato sauce
1-2 teaspoons lime juice
12 corn tortillas

STEPS
1. In a large skillet over medium-high heat, sauté onions in the olive oil for 3-4 minutes, or until almost translucent.

2. Add ground beef, breaking up the beef into pieces with a wooden spoon.

3. Brown until only a little pink color remains. Add garlic, salt, and pepper, and mix them into the meat.

4. Add potatoes and tomato sauce to meat. Stir to combine.

5. Reduce heat to medium and cover. Cook for 20-30 minutes, until potatoes are fork tender. Add 1 teaspoon of lime juice and taste to adjust seasoning, adding additional lime juice if necessary.

6. Warm corn tortillas in the microwave (10-15 seconds on medium heat).

7. Spoon mixture into your tortillas. Serve with salsa, cheese, and sour cream.

SPICY HACK
Add 1 teaspoon of chili powder with the spices in step 3.

NO-MICROWAVE HACK
Warm a skillet over medium heat and heat tortillas for about 1 minute per side, until warm.

How to Pan-Fry

PAN-FRY: Cooking food in a shallow pan filled with just enough fat (typically oil or butter) to cover the bottom. Mostly uses low to medium heat to avoid burning.

TIPS:
• Pan-frying requires both a consistently hot pan and hot oil. Keep the heat no hotter than medium, but ensure that the oil is hot enough to sizzle when you drop in a pinch of flour.
• As with sautéing, don't overcrowd your pan. Not only does this make it difficult to cook your food evenly, but it can cool your oil – a frustrating misstep for pan-frying.
• Keep a paper-towel-lined plate nearby for draining your end result. Skipping this important step will result in your crispy food turning soggy as it sits in the residual oil.

CRISPY CHICKEN

Makes 4 servings.

INGREDIENTS
4 thin-cut boneless, skinless chicken breasts (about ¼-inch thick), or 8 chicken tenders
½ cup all-purpose flour
2 eggs
1 teaspoon Dijon mustard
1½ cups panko or breadcrumbs
1 teaspoon garlic salt (or ½ teaspoon salt and ½ teaspoon garlic powder)
¼ teaspoon pepper
Canola or vegetable oil
Kosher sea salt

STEPS

1. Lay chicken breasts on cutting board. Pat them dry with a paper towel.

2. Create a breading station with three separate parts. Spread flour onto a large plate. In a wide bowl, use a fork to beat together the eggs and Dijon mustard until well mixed. Lastly, on another large plate, combine panko, garlic salt, and pepper.

3. To bread the chicken, press each side into the flour and shake off the excess. Next, dip the floured chicken into the egg mixture, and then move quickly to the panko mixture. Ensure all sides of the chicken are coated.

4. Heat your skillet over medium heat and add a thin (about ¼-inch) layer of oil to the bottom of the pan. You'll know the oil is hot enough by using a trick with the breadcrumbs: throw a pinch of panko into the oil. If it sizzles and turns golden brown in about 15 seconds, it's ready.

5. Cook two chicken breasts in the pan at a time to avoid overcrowding. Fry the chicken for 2 minutes on the first side. Check the doneness by flipping one piece of chicken. If it's golden brown, flip the other chicken breast. If it's not, flip it back over and continue to cook, checking every minute. Repeat with the other side. It should take about 6–8 minutes total to cook the chicken. Repeat with remaining chicken.

6. Sprinkle the chicken with salt immediately after removing it from the oil. Drain chicken on paper towels, and serve hot.

GOURMET HACK
Add ⅛ cup of Parmesan cheese and 1 tablespoon Italian seasoning to the breadcrumbs before breading.

SPICY HACK
Add 1 tablespoon of hot sauce to the egg before breading.

Panko or Breadcrumbs
Breadcrumbs come in a variety of sizes and seasonings. Panko are Japanese breadcrumbs that are light and fluffy and tend to have a larger crumb (if you can't find panko by the breadcrumbs, look in the Asian food section of your supermarket). They make a wonderfully crisp and thick breading. Traditional breadcrumbs tend to have a smaller grain, which results in a thinner layer of breading. They can also be drier, which can occasionally result in a grittier texture. Experiment with each type, and decide which you prefer.

How to Roast

ROAST: Oven-cooking ingredients at a high heat. Creates crispy brown exteriors and moist interiors.

TIPS:
• Roasting is great for everything from meat to vegetables. When using chopped ingredients, cut everything to equal sizes to ensure that everything is cooked evenly.
• Set a timer and follow your nose. Roasting is simple, but you'll want to check the dish at intervals to prevent burning.
• Keep your ingredients uncovered.
• Use the middle rack in your oven, unless the recipe indicates otherwise.

ROASTED ASPARAGUS WITH BALSAMIC BUTTER

Makes 4 servings.

INGREDIENTS
2 pounds asparagus spears
1½ tablespoons olive oil
¼ teaspoon salt
⅛ teaspoon freshly cracked pepper
2 tablespoons salted butter
2 teaspoons balsamic vinegar

STEPS

1. Move the baking rack to the middle position in the oven. Preheat the oven to 400°F.

2. Wash asparagus and pat dry. Cut off the bottom 2 inches of stems.

3. Spread out spears on your baking sheet. Drizzle olive oil over the top of stems, and sprinkle salt and pepper over the asparagus. Use your hands to roll the spears in the oil, making sure each spear is well coated.

4. Roast spears for 8-12 minutes, or until the stalks are tender when pierced with a fork.

5. While asparagus is roasting, melt butter in a small skillet over medium heat. Add balsamic vinegar and whisk until well blended.

6. Drizzle balsamic butter over roasted asparagus until coated.

Prepping Asparagus

The bottom portion of asparagus tends to be woody and difficult to chew. You can usually get rid of this part by cutting off the bottom 2 inches of the stem, but the tough section can vary based on the size and age of the asparagus. To better ensure that you're getting rid of all the tough part, you can also snap off the ends of the asparagus. Simply hold the end of the stalk in one hand and the center of the stalk in the other, and snap the stem. It will naturally break where the woody part ends.

CARAMELIZED ONIONS

Caramelized onions are thinly sliced onions cooked over low heat for a long period of time. The natural sugars in the onions begin to caramelize, which results in a savory, sweet mess of meltingly tender onions. Once you master the technique of caramelizing onions, you can make them in large quantities and keep them in the refrigerator. Dole them out by the spoonful to add their distinct flavor to sauces, eggs, tacos, meat dishes, potatoes, burgers, hot dogs, and sandwiches. They're amazing on grilled cheese sandwiches, like the Gruyère onion grilled cheese recipe on page 105.

Makes about 1 cup onions.

INGREDIENTS
2 sweet onions
1 tablespoon butter
1 tablespoon olive oil
½ teaspoon salt

GOURMET HACK
Add 1 tablespoon of chopped fresh thyme with the onions in step 3. Stir in 1 tablespoon of balsamic vinegar during the last 10 minutes of cooking.

STEPS

1. Heat a pan over medium-low heat. Once warm, add the butter and olive oil, and swirl to coat the pan.

2. While the pan is warming, slice the onions into ⅛-inch slices (see page 25). Add them to the hot pan and toss to coat in the butter. Sprinkle the salt over the onions and toss. Cover the pan.

3. Cook the onions over medium-low heat, stirring every 5–10 minutes, until the onions are soft and brown. If they start to burn or crisp, turn the heat down. Properly caramelized onions take 45–60 minutes to cook.

Not Quite Done o- - - - - - - - ->

Finally Done!

GRUYÈRE ONION GRILLED CHEESE

Makes 1 serving.

INGREDIENTS
2 slices sourdough, French, or Italian bread, about ½-inch thick
About ½ tablespoon of spreadable butter
2 slices Gruyère cheese, or about 1½ ounces
⅛ cup caramelized onions

STEPS

1. Heat frying pan over medium heat for about 5 minutes.

2. Lightly butter both sides of the bread slices.

3. Toast one side of each of the bread slices on the frying pan until golden brown (about 3 minutes).

4. Flip the bread so the toasted side is facing up in the frying pan. Spread the cheese on both bread slices, and place the caramelized onions on one side. Top with the other slice of bread, sandwiching the onions between layers of cheese. The toasted side of the bread should be on the inside, with the untoasted side facing out.

5. Toast until the bottom slice is golden brown (2-3 minutes).

6. When the bottom is golden, use a spatula to flip the sandwich and toast the final side until golden brown (2-3 minutes). Remove from the heat.

7. Cut the sandwiches into quarters and eat!

GOURMET HACK

Rub the cut side of a garlic clove over one side of the sandwich after step 6, just before serving. Add thinly sliced green apples in step 4.

HEARTY HACK

Add crisped bacon slices, shredded pork, or thinly sliced roast beef in step 4.

Cooking with Rice

Rice is a simple ingredient with a lot of potential. It comes in many varieties: white, brown, black, red, jasmine, and more. Rice is easy to cook, easy to store, and serves as a blank slate for any flavors. It's used in almost every culture around the world, in sweet and savory dishes, from breakfast to dessert. It can be the main attraction in recipes like risotto (page 149) and rice pudding, but it's also an economical way to fill your stomach and round out a meal.

Since making rice is specific to the variety, simply follow the package's cooking instructions. Don't be afraid to make extra, because it reheats beautifully in the microwave. (Just add 1 teaspoon of water to the bowl before heating to prevent it from drying out.) On the next page are a few ideas for turning rice into a delicious meal.

Rice Bowls

Top a bowl of rice with roasted meat, grilled fish, steamed vegetables, or a fried egg. It's a great way to use up leftovers when there isn't otherwise enough food to make a full meal.

Soups

Add cooked rice to soup to stretch it into a hearty meal. Try it in chicken soup or as a substitute anywhere you might add pasta. Be aware that the rice will absorb some liquid, however, even when it's precooked.

Chili and Braised Meat

Ladle chili (page 113) or braised food (page 145) over a bowl of rice to let the rice absorb some of the cooking liquid. Rice suddenly becomes a vessel to transfer all of that flavorful broth into your mouth!

Fried Rice

Never throw away leftover rice. It's perfect for making fried rice because some of the moisture has evaporated. A stocked pantry and leftover rice means that you'll always have a delicious meal at your fingertips. Add some soy sauce, chili paste, or hot sauce if you like spicy food, and add whatever leftover protein you have in the refrigerator for a quick treat. Even the simple addition of a scrambled or fried egg can yield a satisfying meal.

How to Fry an Egg

1. Heat a small nonstick skillet with a few tablespoons of oil over medium heat until shimmering.
2. Crack an egg into a separate bowl to make sure there are no eggshells in it and that the yolk is intact.
3. Slowly pour the egg into the oil.
4. Cook the egg for 30-60 seconds, until the bottom of the egg is no longer sticking to the pan.
5. Using the pan's handle, hold the pan at a slight angle over the burner and use a tablespoon to carefully spoon the oil over the top of the egg, until the whites are cooked and no longer clear.
6. It should take 1-2 minutes of basting with the oil until the egg is cooked through. Season with salt and pepper.

BACON FRIED RICE

Makes 2 servings.

INGREDIENTS
2 slices bacon, cut into ¾-inch strips
1 cup leftover cooked rice
2 eggs
1 tablespoon low-sodium soy sauce
½ teaspoon sugar
¼ teaspoon pepper
1 tablespoon vegetable oil
¼ cup frozen mixed vegetables, cooked according to the package

STEPS
1. Heat a medium skillet over medium heat. Add the bacon strips, and fry them in their own fat until crispy. Remove them from the pan and allow them to drain on a paper towel.

2. Add leftover rice to the hot bacon grease. Wait 3 minutes, then flip the rice over. Repeat this process until rice has started to become dry and crispy (about 10–12 minutes).

3. Scramble eggs, soy sauce, sugar, and pepper in a small bowl.

4. Push the rice to the edges of the pan to create an open circle in the center. Add oil to the exposed part of the pan and allow to heat for 30 seconds. Add scrambled-egg mixture to the hot oil, and cook until half-scrambled (the eggs are still wet, but slightly firm). Stir the wet eggs into the rice.

5. Add the cooked vegetables to the skillet and stir to combine, ensuring eggs are cooked through.

6. Serve hot!

GOURMET HACK

Serve with a fried egg on top instead of scrambling the egg.

SPICY HACK

Add chili paste or hot sauce with the egg in step 3.

Rotisserie Chicken Hacks

The rotisserie chicken is one of our favorite shortcuts for weeknight meals. Most major grocery stores sell these precooked chickens ready to go. The meat is usually wonderfully tender and flavorful. Keep an eye on the label though; some chains inject these chickens with artificial flavors and preservatives (if you're concerned about such things).

You can stretch one of these chickens into a few meals. Start by pulling off the skin and discarding it. Now you can take the meat off the bones and use your fingers to shred it. Store the meat in an airtight container in the refrigerator for up to four days, using the meat a little at a time when you want to add chicken to your dishes. Here are a few ideas to get you started:

Salads

Toss ½ cup of warm or cold shredded chicken in a few tablespoons of your favorite salad dressing. Add it to a green salad with tomatoes, cucumbers, and croutons. Make chicken salad for sandwiches by combining 1 cup of shredded chicken with ⅛ cup mayonnaise, 1 teaspoon Dijon mustard, ⅛ cup sliced celery, and salt and pepper.

Soups

There are some really lovely boxed soups that are just shy of a meal. Add ½ cup of warm shredded chicken to your favorite soup and turn it into a heartier meal. You can also add leftover rice or cooked pasta without sauce (smaller shapes, such as orecchiette or stelline, are best) for extra heft. And for those days when all you can muster is some instant ramen, a handful of chicken will make it feel like you put in a little extra effort!

Eggs

Mix ¼ cup of warm chicken into your scrambled eggs toward the end of cooking for a gourmet meal. Add some spinach or mushrooms and a spoonful of salsa to turn it into a dinner-worthy dish.

Tacos or Nachos

Add a spoonful of your favorite salsa to ½ cup of chicken and heat it up. Serve on tortillas or nacho chips with your favorite Mexican cheese blend, sliced avocados, and sour cream. Tacos and nachos are also great with beans, if you have any on hand.

Pasta

Spaghetti and jarred cream sauce get a makeover when you top them with shredded chicken. Suddenly you have chicken alfredo instead of just pasta with cream sauce.

Roommate Food Swap

A food swap is a fun way to make sure you have healthy, delicious homemade meals for lunch or dinner.

Here's how it works: You and your roommates spend an evening in the kitchen making recipes that can be reheated and used throughout the week. Maybe one roommate takes a main course, another takes vegetables, and another takes dessert or cleanup duty. Rotate the jobs weekly, and everyone gets to try new recipes and explore new food. Divvy up the food for lunches, or save it for a roommate dinner on a busy weeknight when no one has time to cook.

There are certain foods that reheat better than others, so look for recipes that will keep in the refrigerator for three to four days. Here are a few ideas:

- baked or roasted chicken
- soups or stews
- meatballs
- braised meat
- mashed potatoes
- sautéed greens
- steamed vegetables

BEAN CHILI

This bean chili recipe is so hearty that you won't even notice it's vegetarian. It gets even better on the second and third days, so make a big batch and reheat it throughout the week. Serve it over rice or mashed potatoes to get more meals out of it. It will keep for up to five days in the refrigerator.

Makes 6 servings.

INGREDIENTS
1 tablespoon vegetable oil
1 small onion, chopped
1 clove garlic, minced
2 tablespoons chili powder
2 16-ounce cans black beans, drained and rinsed
1 16-ounce can kidney beans, drained and rinsed
1 14.5-ounce or 16-ounce can tomato sauce
Optional toppings for serving: sour cream, Mexican cheese blend,
   chopped cilantro, lime wedges

STEPS
1. Heat the vegetable oil in a large pot over medium-high heat.

2. Add the onion and cook until translucent (3–4 minutes). Add the garlic and chili powder, and sauté until the garlic is lightly browned and fragrant (about 90 seconds).

3. Add the beans and tomato sauce and bring to a simmer. Cook until beans are warmed through, about 10 minutes.

4. Serve in bowls and let people add their own toppings, if using.

GOURMET HACK
Add ½ tablespoon of cumin and 1 teaspoon of coriander with the chili powder in step 2.

HEARTY HACK
Add one bag of frozen corn with the beans.

SPICY HACK
Add ½ tablespoon of dried chipotle pepper with the chili powder in step 2.

Pizza Hacks and DIY Pizza Bars

Making pizza is a fun and easy way to cook dinner for yourself or for a crowd. One of our favorite simple dinner-party ideas is to set out ingredients like the ones listed on the next page, so that everyone can assemble their favorite combo. Another bonus – the variety of ingredients means you can still enjoy your pepperoni, even if your roommates are vegetarian!

The Base

You can find premade pizza dough in any grocery store. Prepare it according to the package's instructions, add your toppings, and bake! If you really want to cut corners, you can also buy precooked crust. Don't be afraid to get creative. English muffins, pitas, flatbreads, and tortillas all make great stand-in pizza crusts.

The Sauce

A jar of pizza sauce is always great to keep on hand, but you can also use the little bit of marinara sauce that's left in the can from pasta night. And don't stop with red sauce! Try pesto, alfredo sauce, or even barbecue sauce.

The Cheese

Look for softer cheese blends that melt easily, such as mozzarella, Gruyère, or fontina. Harder cheeses won't give you the same gooey effect, but they're equally delicious. Feta and Parmesan won't melt in the same way, but they still have their place!

The Toppings

The sky's the limit when it comes to pizza toppings. Cured meats such as pepperoni and salami are traditional, but shredded pork, leftover chicken breast, or bacon crumbles can all make amazing pizza toppings. To make it easier on yourself, stick to vegetables that don't need to be cooked first, and thinly slice the crispier ones (such as onions, mushrooms, and zucchini). We love fresh corn, halved cherry tomatoes, and sliced green onions. Keep jars of black or green olives, pickled jalapenos, capers, or roasted red peppers in the fridge, since they have long shelf lives. Don't forget the herbs and spices! Italian seasoning, dried oregano, red pepper flakes, and fresh basil can make your homemade pizza special.

Cooking

If you buy premade dough, the package will have instructions for how to cook the pizza.

For English muffins, pitas, flatbreads, and tortillas, preheat your oven or your toaster oven's broiler to 400°F (medium setting). Place the base on a foil-lined baking sheet and add the toppings. Broil for 3–7 minutes, until the cheese is melted, but before the edges start to burn.

You can really get creative with your pizzas, and here are a few ideas to get you started:

- English muffin + pizza sauce + mozzarella cheese + sliced pepperoni + sliced black olives

- Pita + feta cheese + sliced Kalamata olives + thinly sliced red onion + halved cherry tomatoes + oregano

- Flour tortilla + barbecue sauce + Gruyère cheese + shredded rotisserie chicken + sliced green onions

- Flatbread + pesto + fontina cheese + fresh corn

Salads without Greens

Salads don't always have to have greens in them. As long as you find a substitute for the crunch that salad greens provide, you can make something delicious and healthy without lettuce. Cucumbers, carrots, celery, and cabbage are all great options to add that satisfying crunch to a dish.

TOMATO CUCUMBER SALAD

Makes 4 servings.

INGREDIENTS
1 cup cherry tomatoes, halved, or 1 large tomato, diced
1 English cucumber
1 ball of mozzarella cheese
2 tablespoons balsamic vinaigrette (page 17)

STEPS
1. Cut the cucumber into ¼-inch slices, and cut the slices into quarters.

2. Slice the ball of mozzarella into ½-inch cubes.

3. Combine the tomatoes, cucumber, cheese, and balsamic vinaigrette in a large bowl. Toss to combine.

GOURMET HACK
Top with fresh chopped basil.

HEARTY HACK
Add grilled chicken and serve over greens.

Dessert for a Crowd

The obvious choices when baking for a crowd are pies, cakes, and cookies, but sometimes it's fun to surprise people with a spin on a classic dish. Pie chips are simply sheets of pie dough cut into small pieces and baked until golden brown. You can treat them like chips and dip by serving them with a sweet sauce similar to a pie filling.

PIE CHIPS WITH BERRY DIP

Makes 4 servings.

Pie Chips

INGREDIENTS
2 premade pie crusts
1 egg
1 tablespoon water
4 tablespoons turbinado sugar (large crystals of brown sugar)
Nonstick cooking spray

GOURMET HACK

Sprinkle with cinnamon sugar (page 92) instead of turbinado sugar in step 4.

STEPS

1. Preheat an oven to 350°F. Spray a light layer of nonstick cooking spray over a baking sheet.

2. Unroll the pie crusts. Use a round cookie cutter to cut out circles of pie dough, or use a knife to cut 2-inch squares of dough. Place on a baking sheet with ½ inch between the pieces.

3. Make an egg wash to help the pastry brown evenly. Crack the egg into a small bowl, and add the water to the egg. Beat well with a fork.

4. Use a pastry brush to brush the egg wash over the pie crusts. Sprinkle the sugar over the rounds.

5. Bake for 9–14 minutes, until the pie chips are golden brown. These can be made up to one day in advance and stored in an airtight container.

6. Serve with the berry dip (below), dipping the chips into the fruit.

Berry Dip

INGREDIENTS
1 cup mixed frozen berries
¼ cup sugar
1 tablespoon lemon juice
1 teaspoon cornstarch

GOURMET HACK

Experiment with different types of fruit, such as apples, cranberries, mangoes, and peaches.

STEPS

1. Heat a small saucepan over medium-high heat.

2. Add the berries, sugar, and lemon juice to the pan.

3. Heat and stir often until the berries begin to soften and bubble (about 5 minutes). Sprinkle the cornstarch over the berries, and stir to mix. Continue to cook until the sauce starts to thicken (about 5 minutes longer).

The Big Game Party

Have a big group of friends over to cheer on your favorite team. Don't be intimidated by cooking for a crowd, and don't resort to ordering pizza! If you're overwhelmed, turn it into a potluck and ask everyone to bring something to share.

The Menu

Tomato cucumber salad
DIY pizza bar
Pie chips with berry dip

FUN HACK

Add food dye in your team's colors to a container of cream cheese frosting to serve with the pie chips.

CELEBRATION HACK

Hold a contest for the most creative pizza design representing your team.

FIRST SOLO KITCHEN

You've made it to your own kitchen! More space, a full (conflict-free!) refrigerator, and the ability to cook whenever you want. You already know how to build a great pantry, full of both essentials and your own personal favorites. This chapter builds on your experience and guides you through more advanced concepts. In addition to learning a few new techniques, you'll also explore how to tweak a recipe to match your palate and how to introduce the flavors of your favorite cuisines into a dish.

We both fondly remember our first kitchens. Alyssa saved for a year to buy her fancy Dutch oven (which she was able to get on sale in her favorite color — whoo!). Carla mixed all her cookie and cake batters with a wooden spoon for years until she finally got her stand mixer. These purchases are the types that really make a kitchen feel like your own!

Saving v. Splurging

Living in your first solo apartment is a balancing act. You want to save money, but you also don't want to live like a college student anymore. There are a few items worth spending the extra cash on, but in some cases, you're just paying for a brand name or packaging. Here are some tips to guide you through learning how to spend your hard-earned cash.

BULK BINS

The bulk bins are a great place to save money. Many natural or organic grocery stores have sections with huge bins of pasta, beans, cereal, and spices. You can buy just as much as you need and reduce food waste, and you can try new ingredients without committing to large quantities. On the other hand, if you consume a lot of cereal or pasta every week, it's worth buying it in bulk to save money. Just be sure to transfer any purchases from the bulk bin into an airtight container once you get home, to keep your ingredients as fresh as possible and extend their shelf lives.

WAREHOUSE CLUBS

Membership-only warehouse clubs are another way to buy in bulk and save money, especially if you're often cooking for a crowd. Try to focus on the less perishable items such as frozen foods, cooking oils, baking supplies, rice, and beverages. That giant crate of strawberries might look delicious and seem like a great idea, but you might have a hard time getting through them before they go bad. Of course, freezing produce is always an option.

PRODUCE

Many grocery stores will have a table or section of produce that's a few days from expiring. If you know you're going to consume something immediately, take advantage of that section. Just be sure to check everything for mold and rot before purchasing, because it's worth spending a few extra pennies to avoid getting sick!

FROZEN FOODS

Certain food is cheaper, easier, and higher quality when frozen. Peas and corn tend to be flash-frozen at the peak of their season for optimum flavor, and you save yourself the trouble of shelling countless pea pods. Frozen vegetable medleys are great additions to soups, stir-fries, and fried rice.

MEAT, FISH, AND CHEESE

There are definitely ingredients for which cheaper is not necessarily better. You don't want to take risks with meat and fish. High-quality cheeses taste worlds better than the cheaper stuff, and there's no substitute for freshly grated Parmesan (which tastes very different from the canned version). Be discerning about what brands of spices you buy, because the cheaper spices are more likely to carry harmful bacteria, such as salmonella, and can be less potent.

First Solo Kitchen Pantry

At this point, you've got the basic pantry covered. You're looking for some special ingredients that can really take your cooking from great to fantastic. Some of these are more perishable, but they're versatile ingredients that you can use in many dishes. As you learn what you like to cook and eat, your list will evolve and grow.

RISOTTO RICE (ARBORIO, CARNAROLI)

Preparing risotto sounds fancy, but it's really just a way to cook incredibly flavorful rice. It's easy to adjust to feed a group of people, and it is perfect to help use up any leftovers from the fridge or any vegetables that are a few days away from the compost bin.

HIGH-QUALITY PARMESAN CHEESE OR PECORINO ROMANO CHEESE

A sprinkle of freshly grated Parmesan or Pecorino Romano can add saltiness and depth of flavor to almost any savory dish. Add it to soups and stews, rice dishes, eggs, pasta, meat, potatoes, and roasted vegetables. Save the hard edges (the rinds) in the freezer and add them to sauces, soups, stews, risotto, chili, and anything that needs to simmer for a long time. The cheese will slowly infuse your dish with subtle flavor.

WONTON WRAPPERS

You can fill wonton wrappers with practically anything! Roll them around shrimp, stuff them with minced meat and vegetables, or just fry them on their own and use them as chips. You can find them in the refrigerated section near the produce (usually by the tofu). If you don't use them, freeze them within a few days and thaw before using.

PESTO AND TAPENADE

Pesto is a puree made from basil, pine nuts, Italian cheese, and olive oil. Tapenade is a chunky mixture usually made from olives and olive oil. It can include other ingredients as well, such as garlic or sun-dried tomatoes. Both condiments are delicious mixed in pasta, spread on crostini (see page 130) or crackers, used as a substitute for pizza sauce, added to meats, or tossed with roasted vegetables.

SMOKED SEA SALT

Smoked sea salt is what would happen if bacon and salt got together and had a baby. It's exactly what it sounds like — flaky sea salt that has been smoked. It's an amazing addition to chilis, soups, stews, popcorn, sauces, meat, seafood, potatoes, and roasted vegetables. And if you're vegetarian, the smoky flavor is a good way to fake a hint of bacon in a dish.

HERBES DE PROVENCE

Herbes de Provence is a dried herb mix that includes a variety of common French herbs, such as lavender, oregano, thyme, and rosemary. It's a delicate blend that enhances chicken, fish, and vegetables.

PERISHABLE ITEMS
Other highly perishable items can add depth and finesse to your cooking.

• Keep fresh lemons and limes on hand for both their juice and their zest. The juice can add brightness to any recipe that tastes too heavy and rich, while the zest adds a more delicate flavor, but a strong scent and beautiful color, to a dish.

• Fresh herbs can make a basic dish come alive. Use hardier herbs such as rosemary, thyme, and sage at the beginning of cooking so they can slowly release their oils and infuse a dish with flavor. It's best to add the more tender herbs – such as basil, parsley, and cilantro – at the end of cooking or as a garnish, so they don't discolor or get lost in the more dominant flavors of a dish.

• Fresh ginger has a distinct spiciness that mellows as it cooks. The flavor is warm and bright and a great addition to savory and sweet recipes.

Remember, it's best to start with small amounts of any seasonings or spices and gradually add more when necessary. As you gain experience in the kitchen, you'll become more comfortable adjusting ingredients for a fantastic final dish.

First Solo Kitchen Equipment

Finally! You have space and you don't have to share it. The best way to begin to stock those shelves is to expand into specialized tools. As you peruse recipes, start to jot down the recommended equipment and keep a list of items that keep coming up. The following list is a great place to start.

MICROPLANE

A microplane grater is perfect for zesting citrus fruits, as well as grating items like ginger, garlic, and even small portions of cheese. Microplane graters are sharp, so look for one with a cover for the blades and a sturdy rubber handle for a safe grip.

SCALE

Many recipes call for weight measurements (like ounces) instead of volume recipes (like tablespoons). Digital scales are inexpensive, precise, and easy to use.

COOLING RACK

Small and easily stored, cooking racks allow you to cool items easily and efficiently by allowing airflow on all sides of the food. Start with a single cooling rack. If you find yourself baking often, you can invest in something more elaborate.

FOOD PROCESSOR

If you love cooking large portions for leftovers or parties, the chopping, grating and blending capabilities of this appliance are perfect for you. While these machines can take up quite a bit of space, they are fantastic for reducing the time involved with meal prep. Buy the largest size you can comfortably store, and make sure it comes with metal attachments and a blade for every function you will need.

MANDOLIN

If you regularly slice items like potatoes and onions, this simple tool has the capacity to make your life much, much easier. Mandolins specialize in creating very thin, uniform slices of food for dishes. Consider investing in a safety glove to make sure you don't have any accidents.

RICE COOKER

You already know how versatile rice is in the kitchen (page 107). The next step for this nutritious staple is a rice cooker, a small appliance that easily cooks your rice without supervision and then keeps it warm until you are ready to eat it.

DEEP-FRY AND CANDY THERMOMETER

When deep-frying, the best way to be sure that your oil is at the optimum temperature is to use a thermometer. A combo thermometer for both deep-fry oil and candy is a great option. Making candy like caramel is easier than you might think once you own a candy thermometer. Select a thermometer with a digital display; these are inexpensive and readily available.

ENAMELED CAST-IRON DUTCH OVEN

This is a versatile piece you can use either on the stovetop or in the oven. It retains heat evenly for hours, is easy to clean, and also makes a lovely serving vessel. When buying, look for a heavy, lidded Dutch oven with no chips in the enamel. For safety, make sure the handles on the sides and lid are large enough to grasp securely when using potholders. And do some brand research to find what is best for you. Find a piece with a long enamel warranty from a highly rated company.

Advanced Techniques and Recipes

Seasoning to Taste

Seasoning is the ultimate hack. Recipes are a great way to practice techniques and learn how to cook, but they're usually written by one person with a specific idea of how they think the dish should taste. As you become more confident in the kitchen, you'll be able to taste a dish and identify ways that you can make it more suited to your taste. When you taste your food, ask yourself a few questions to decide how to adjust the flavors.

1. Does it need salt? When used properly, salt should enhance the flavors of a dish without making it taste salty. Only add a little bit at a time when cooking, because you can always add more salt, but you can't take it away. Certain foods are just generally salty, such as Parmesan cheese, soy sauce, bacon, mustard, miso paste, and hot sauce. You can use them to add more complex flavor than salt alone can provide.

2. Does it need pepper? Black pepper can lend warm liveliness to a dish, or a larger quantity can make things fairly spicy. People have varying levels of tolerance for black pepper, so recipes tend to err on the low side. If you find that a dish could use a tiny kick, add a little more pepper.

3. Does it need acid? Sweetness? Balancing the acidity of a dish with its richness or sweetness takes practice, but it can make food sing in your mouth. Think about adding a squeeze of fresh lemon or lime, a splash of vinegar, or even a hint of citrus zest. If a dish is bordering on too acidic, a sprinkle of sugar or a hint of honey can balance out the sourness.

4. Are the flavors strong enough? If it feels like something is missing, sometimes you just need to add a little more of whatever herbs and spices were included in the recipe.

Fancy Toast

Crostini is the Italian word for "toasted baguette slices." These slices have a wide variety of uses and are easy to make. You can pile all sorts of amazing things on them, from savory to sweet, and serve them at parties as a delicious classic appetizer.

The Bread

Start with a fresh loaf of crusty Italian bread or a French baguette. Use a bread knife to cut the bread into slices (about ½-inch thick), or have the bakery do it for you. Toast lightly, until the outside is slightly crisp and just starting to brown, but before it becomes golden brown. If using an oven, preheat to 300°F and spread your slices on a baking sheet. Bake for 3 minutes, then flip the slices and continue to bake for about 3–5 more minutes. You can make crostini up to one day in advance and store them in airtight containers once they've cooled.

BAKED BRIE

Makes 6 servings.

INGREDIENTS
About 5 ounces Brie cheese
⅛ cup your favorite jam (try apricot or fig)
Nonstick cooking spray
Crostini for serving (page 130)

STEPS
1. Preheat the oven to 350°F.

2. Spray an oven-safe dish with nonstick spray.

3. Place the Brie in the dish and spread the jam over the top of the cheese.

4. Bake for 20–30 minutes, until the jam is melted and the cheese is soft. It may not look pretty, but it will be delicious!

5. Serve hot with crostini.

GOURMET HACK

Top with ⅛ cup of chopped walnuts. Make crostini with raisin bread. Substitute Camembert for the Brie. You can also substitute crackers or flatbread for the crostini.

TRADITIONAL BRUSCHETTA

Makes 4 servings.

INGREDIENTS
1 large ripe tomato, or about 16 cherry tomatoes
1 clove garlic, peeled and minced
2 tablespoons high-quality extra virgin olive oil
½ teaspoon sea salt
¼ teaspoon pepper
8 crostini (page 130)
1½ tablespoons freshly chopped basil (about 6 leaves)

GOURMET HACK
Add 1 teaspoon balsamic vinegar or small cubes of mozzarella to the bowl in step 1. Cut the basil into a chiffonade (page 142) if you're feeling fancy.

STEPS
1. Chop the tomato into a ½-inch dice, or cut cherry tomatoes in half. Transfer the tomato and any juices to a medium bowl. Add the minced garlic, olive oil, salt, and pepper. Mix to combine.

2. Chop the basil leaves.

3. Divide the tomato mixture among your toasts and top with the basil.

BLUE CHEESE AND HONEY CROSTINI

Makes 4 servings.

INGREDIENTS
8 tablespoons crumbled blue cheese
8 lightly toasted crostini (page 130)
4 tablespoons honey

GOURMET HACK
Sprinkle ½ tablespoon of chopped walnuts over each slice before serving.

STEPS
1. Move the rack in your oven to the top setting. Preheat the broiler to 400°F (medium setting).

2. Place the crostini on a baking sheet. Place 1 tablespoon of blue cheese on each baguette slice.

3. Put the baking sheet under the broiler and broil for 3–5 minutes, until the cheese is melted but before the crostini start to burn.

4. Remove the crostini from the oven and drizzle ½ tablespoon of honey over each slice.

RICOTTA AND OLIVE OIL CROSTINI

Makes 4 servings.

INGREDIENTS
¾ cup ricotta cheese
4 tablespoons high-quality extra virgin olive oil
8 crostini (page 130)
2 teaspoons kosher sea salt

STEPS

1. Use a spoon to spread about 1½ tablespoons of ricotta cheese on each slice of bread.

2. Drizzle about ½ tablespoon of olive oil over each slice. Sprinkle with about ¼ teaspoon of salt.

GOURMET HACK

Top with lemon zest or chopped fresh basil.

Crostini with Salad

You can take this new fancy toast knowledge and use it to turn lighter dishes into a full meal. This fairly basic salad gets a French twist when you add a goat-cheese crostini with a sprinkle of herbs. Suddenly you have a delicious lunch or a fancier salad course.

FRENCH GOAT CHEESE SALAD

Makes 4 servings.

INGREDIENTS
1 recipe lemon mustard vinaigrette (page 55)
4 cups baby lettuce
1 cup halved cherry tomatoes
8 1-inch slices of baguette
1 log or 6 ounces goat cheese with a rind (look for the words *boucheron*,
  soft ripened, or *chevre blanc* on the label; you don't want the really soft,
  crumbly kind of fresh chevre)
2 tablespoons Herbes de Provence

STEPS
1. Wash the greens in a colander and thoroughly dry them. You can air-dry them, or use a clean towel or a salad spinner to speed up the process.

2. Place the greens in a large bowl. Add a little bit of the dressing, and use your hands to gently coat the greens. Add more dressing until the greens are lightly coated. Taste, and adjust salt and pepper as necessary. Top with tomatoes, and set aside.

3. Preheat your oven's broiler on medium heat and place your oven rack on the highest position.

4. Cut the goat cheese log into eight equal slices. Place the baguette slices on a baking sheet and top each one with a slice of cheese. Sprinkle the Herbes de Provence over the cheese.

5. Broil the bread and cheese for about 3 minutes, until the cheese is melted and the rind is starting to brown. Remove from the oven. Serve warm with the lettuce.

HEARTY HACK

Add leftover roasted chicken or grilled chicken breast, sliced avocado, or sliced cucumber to the salad.

How to Deep Fry

DEEP FRY:
A method of cooking in which you heat a deep layer of oil to around 400°F, submerge an ingredient in the hot oil, and cook to achieve a crisp exterior.

TIPS:

• Use a thermometer to maintain consistent oil temperature.

• Cook larger pieces of food at lower temperatures so the outside doesn't burn before the inside is done.

• Adding too much food at one time will crowd the pan, causing the temperature of the oil to drop dramatically, and your ingredients won't fry properly.

• You can reuse frying oil several times before it goes bad. Just filter out any food particles and store in a large glass jar or the empty original container. It will smell off when it's gone bad.

• Don't pour oil down the sink — ever! It might seem like an easy shortcut, but it will wreak havoc on your plumbing. Wait for it to cool, then transfer it to a biodegradable container and add it to your compost bin. No compost bin? Seal it in a jar to throw it away.

WONTON CHIPS

Makes 8 servings.

INGREDIENTS
Vegetable or canola oil
30 small wonton wrappers
Kosher sea salt

GOURMET HACK
Sprinkle black or white toasted sesame seeds with the salt in step 4.

STEPS

1. Pour 1 inch of oil into a large, high-sided saucepan over medium-high heat. Heat for about 5 minutes.

2. Test that the oil is ready for frying by adding a wonton wrapper. If the wrapper sizzles and starts to puff up, it's ready.

3. Add 3-4 wonton wrappers to the oil (so they don't touch each other). Fry for about 90 seconds on one side, until golden brown. Flip and fry the other side for about 60 seconds. You want them to turn golden brown but not get too dark.

4. Use tongs to pull the wontons out of the oil and drain on a paper towel. Sprinkle salt on the wontons immediately.

5. Repeat until you have fried all of the wontons.

6. The wontons can be fried up to one day in advance and kept in an airtight container. Serve with cheesy spinach dip (page 141).

Smoke Point

The smoke point is the temperature at which oil starts to smoke and break down. You should avoid heating oil to this point. Refined oils like safflower, sunflower, canola, and corn oil have higher smoke points and tend to be more affordable, which makes them ideal for deep-frying. Olive oil, nut oils, unrefined oils, and butter generally have lower smoke points, and are better suited to cooking at lower temperatures.

CHEESY SPINACH DIP

Makes 8 servings.

INGREDIENTS
10 ounces frozen spinach, thawed
8 ounces cream cheese, at room temperature
½ cup ricotta cheese
¾ cup of your favorite shredded Italian cheese blend, reserving ¼ cup
½ teaspoon garlic salt
½ teaspoon kosher sea salt
¼ teaspoon pepper

STEPS

1. Preheat the oven to 400°F.

2. Squeeze as much moisture out of the spinach as you can. Chop the spinach into small pieces.

3. Combine all of the ingredients in a large bowl, except for the reserved Italian cheese. Mix well.

4. Transfer the mixture to a medium oven-safe dish. Top with the reserved Italian cheese.

5. Bake for 35–45 minutes, until the cheese is melted and the edges are bubbly.

6. Serve with wonton chips (page 140).

GOURMET HACK
Add half a can of chopped artichoke hearts in step 3.

First Solo Kitchen Knife Skills

Chiffonade

A chiffonade creates thin, light strips of leafy herbs or greens. It's commonly used for basil or mint. Stack 3-6 washed and dried leaves on top of each other.

Roll tightly into a tube shape.

Start at one end of the tube and cut very thin slices, at least $1/16$ inch thick.

Chopping and Mincing Herbs

To use herbs in cooking, wash and dry them. For hardy herbs such as rosemary and thyme, you will need to strip the leaves from the woody stems, which are too tough to eat. You can eat the stems of more tender herbs such as cilantro and parsley, but recipes generally call for only the parts near the leaves.

Place the stripped herbs in a pile in the center of your cutting board.

Use a rocking motion with your knife to cut through the pile and chop the herbs into smaller pieces. Keep mounding the pile and cutting until the herbs are the desired size. Chopped herbs are in larger pieces, usually around ¼ inch in size. Minced herbs are much smaller, around $\frac{1}{16}$ of an inch – basically as small as you can get them with your knife.

How to Braise

BRAISE:
A method in which you brown an ingredient in oil, add liquid to the pot, and cook over low heat until tender. Common braising liquids are water, stock, and wine. It's an excellent way to turn tough cuts of meat into tender, rich meals.

TIPS:
• Use a heavy-bottomed pot, such as an enameled cast-iron Dutch oven.

• The key to getting a good sear on food is to put it in the pan and not touch it. If you try to turn your meat in the pan and it's stuck, it's probably not ready yet. Let it sit until it has a nice crust (but don't let it burn!).

• After browning your meat or vegetables, you'll have little bits of caramelized food stuck to the bottom of the pan. These are full of flavor. When you add the braising liquid, use a spoon or spatula to scrape these pieces off the bottom of the pan.

• Cover the pot while simmering to prevent the liquid from evaporating.

HERB BRAISED PORK

Ladle this tender pork and rich broth over herbed rice pilaf (page 150), mashed potatoes, grits, or polenta. Or add extra chicken stock and 1 cup of beans to turn it into a rich soup, and serve it with crusty, buttered French bread. This recipe tastes even better the next few days, so don't be afraid to make extra!

When purchasing your pork, note that pork shoulder and pork butt are the same cut of meat, so you can buy either.

Makes 8 servings.

INGREDIENTS
2½ pounds pork shoulder or butt, cut into 1-inch cubes
1 tablespoon olive oil
1 onion, chopped
1 carrot, cut into a ¼-inch dice
2 cloves garlic, chopped
1 tablespoon chopped rosemary
1 tablespoon chopped thyme
3 cups chicken stock

HEALTHY HACK
Use whole pieces of skin-on chicken breasts, thighs, and legs instead of pork, and cook for about 60-90 minutes.

GOURMET HACK
Add a few Parmesan rinds in step 7. Remove before serving.

STEPS

1. Heat the oil in a large, heavy pot over medium-high heat.

2. Brown the pork cubes in batches. Place as many cubes in the pot as can comfortably fit with about 1 inch of space around each piece. Cook for 2-3 minutes, until a brown crust has formed. Flip the cubes and brown the other side for 2-3 minutes. Remove the browned pork and place it on a plate or in a bowl. Repeat until all of the pork is browned. Be careful not to burn yourself on oil popping up out of the pan.

3. Drain most of the oil, leaving a thin layer in the bottom of the pan.

4. Add the onion and carrot. Cook, stirring often, until the onion is translucent. Scrape the bottom of the pot as you stir to pull up any browned bits of meat that stuck to the pot. This should take 3-5 minutes.

5. Add the garlic and cook for another 3 minutes, stirring often.

6. Add the herbs and cook for 1 minute, stirring often.

7. Add the pork and any accumulated juices back to the pot. Add the chicken stock and bring to a boil over high heat. Reduce to a simmer and cover.

8. Stir approximately every 30 minutes to make sure the low simmer is maintained and that none of the vegetables are sticking to the bottom of the pot. Simmer until the pork is fork-tender (about 2-4 hours, depending on your cut of meat).

Fancy Rice

Rice absorbs flavor while it cooks, and there are different techniques and cooking liquids you can use to take rice to the next level. Risotto is an Italian rice dish that transforms rice into a creamy, rich meal. Herbs and chicken stock make rice pilaf a flavorful side dish.

Traditionally, preparing a risotto is a time-intensive project that involves babysitting the pot and adding liquid by the spoonful. This method is much easier but yields results that are just as delicious!

BACON AND PEA RISOTTO

Makes 2 servings.

GOURMET HACK
Grate a dusting of lemon zest over the final dish.

INGREDIENTS
1 teaspoon olive oil
4 slices bacon
1 cup Arborio or Carnaroli rice
4 cups chicken stock
1 cup frozen peas
½ cup Parmesan cheese
For serving: Add an additional ½ cup Parmesan cheese, and pass the pepper mill for people to add their own seasoning.

STEPS

1. Heat the oil in a large, heavy-bottomed pot over medium-high heat. Cut the bacon into ¼-inch matchsticks and fry until crisp, about 5–7 minutes.

2. Remove the bacon from the pot and drain on a paper towel. Set aside. Remove all but 1 tablespoon of oil from the pot. Return the pot to medium-high heat.

3. Add the rice and cook, stirring often, for 2 minutes.

4. Add the stock and peas to the pot. Bring to a boil over high heat, then reduce immediately to a low simmer.

5. Cook the rice, stirring often and scraping the bottom of the pan to make sure the rice doesn't stick. The rice is done when it is tender and has absorbed most of the liquid. It should take 25–35 minutes, and your rice will be suspended in a creamy, glossy liquid. If you run out of stock before the rice is cooked, add more warm stock or water, ½ cup at a time.

6. When the rice is cooked, remove from the heat and stir in the Parmesan cheese and bacon. Taste and add salt or pepper if necessary. Serve immediately with extra cheese and pepper.

HERBED RICE PILAF

Makes 6 servings.

INGREDIENTS
2 tablespoons olive oil
1 medium onion, chopped
½ teaspoon kosher sea salt
2 cups uncooked rice medley (mixed rice)
Chicken stock (replace the amount of water or stock called for on the rice package's cooking instructions with chicken stock, probably about 4 cups)
¼ cup chopped parsley
Serve with herb braised pork (page 146) or roasted chicken

STEPS
1. Heat the oil in a large heavy pot over medium-high heat.

2. Add the chopped onion and salt, and cook until translucent (about 3–4 minutes).

3. Add the rice and toast, stirring often, for about 4 minutes.

4. Add the chicken stock and bring to a boil. Cover and reduce to a low simmer. Finish cooking until rice is tender and most of the liquid has been absorbed. This can take anywhere from 20–50 minutes, depending on what kind of rice you use. Reference the cooking instructions on the rice's packaging for guidelines.

5. When the rice is done cooking, add the parsley to the pot and toss to combine.

GOURMET HACK
Add 1 tablespoon of lemon zest with the parsley. Sauté a chopped red bell pepper with the onion in step 2.

Exploring Different Cuisines

As you try different recipes, travel more extensively, and dine in restaurants more often, you'll find yourself drawn to certain flavors and cuisines. Some people never get sick of Indian food, while others love the flavors of Japan. One of the beautiful things about cooking for yourself is that you can incorporate your favorite flavors into any recipe.

Herbs, spices, cheeses, and condiments are the easiest ways to evoke the cooking of a certain region, and you can easily add them to hack existing recipes and give them their own flair. For example, you can give the bacon and pea risotto recipe (page 149) a French makeover by adding shallots and goat cheese. Or you can make it more Italian by substituting the bacon with pancetta and adding fresh basil before serving.

Here are some popular worldwide cuisines and their signature flavors. It's worth noting that every country has specialized dishes by region, and these are just a few suggestions.

FRENCH

Savory: tarragon, lavender, thyme, shallots, mustard, butter, goat cheese, Brie cheese, blue cheese

Sweet: lavender, almond extract, honey, goat cheese, butter

INDIAN

Savory: coriander, cumin, curry powder, turmeric, cardamom, star anise, ginger, garlic, tomatoes, yogurt

Sweet: ginger, anise, cardamom, cinnamon, cloves, coconut, almond, pistachios, mango

MEXICAN

Savory: chili powder, oregano, jalapeno, chipotle peppers in adobo sauce, lime, cilantro, cinnamon, cocoa

Sweet: cinnamon, cocoa, honey, caramel, cream

ITALIAN

Savory: basil, rosemary, garlic, fennel, capers, lemon, olive oil, balsamic vinegar, tomatoes, olives, mozzarella cheese, Parmesan cheese, ricotta cheese, cured meat (prosciutto, pancetta)

Sweet: anise, hazelnut, vanilla, chocolate, orange, lemon, honey, coffee, balsamic vinegar

JAPANESE

Savory: ginger, sesame, soy sauce, wasabi, dashi, rice vinegar

Sweet: green tea, yuzu, red bean paste (azuki), fresh fruit

SOUTHEAST ASIAN

Savory: lime, ginger, mint, lemongrass, curry paste, fish sauce, soy sauce, coconut milk, peanuts, cucumber

Sweet: mint, cane sugar, coconut, peanuts, mango, fresh fruit

TERIYAKI SALMON

Teriyaki is a salty, sweet, savory sauce. You can buy it in the supermarket, but it's easy to make yourself and is much tastier when homemade. Make extra to keep in the refrigerator for up to one week, and reuse for other meals.

Makes 4 servings.

INGREDIENTS
For the sauce:
1 cup low-sodium soy sauce
½ cup brown sugar
¼ tablespoon honey
2 tablespoons cornstarch
2 tablespoons mirin (seasoned rice wine)
2 cloves garlic, minced
1 tablespoon minced ginger

For the salmon:
4 salmon fillets
Nonstick spray
Optional: 1 tablespoon toasted sesame seeds,
  2 tablespoons chopped scallions

BUDGET HACK
Replace the salmon with chicken and cook at 400°F for 18–25 minutes, until the center is no longer pink.

HEARTY HACK
Serve over rice for a more filling meal.

STEPS

1. Combine all the sauce ingredients in a small saucepan over medium heat.

2. Bring to a boil, then reduce to a simmer, stirring often, for 10 minutes.

4. Raise the oven rack to the highest position. Preheat your oven's broiler to medium heat or 400°F.

5. Line a baking sheet with tinfoil, and spray with nonstick cooking spray. Place the salmon fillets skin-side down on the foil. Spoon ¼ cup of the teriyaki sauce over each fillet.

6. Broil for 3 minutes. Remove the tray from the oven and flip the salmon over. Divide the remaining teriyaki sauce among the fillets and return the salmon to the oven. Broil for 4-5 minutes longer, until the center of the fish is cooked through.

7. Transfer the fish to a plate and top with the sesame seeds or scallions, if using.

Fresh Ginger

Fresh ginger is warm and spicy, with more bite than its dried counterpart. Look for it in the produce aisle. Avoid ginger that looks dried out or shriveled. To prep fresh ginger, cut a knob from the larger piece. Use the edge of a spoon to scrape off the skin. Use a chef's knife to mince the ginger or cut it into smaller pieces, and press it with a garlic press. Store fresh ginger in the refrigerator.

SESAME GREEN BEANS

Makes 4 servings.

1 pound green beans, washed and ends trimmed
2 tablespoons sesame oil
1 tablespoon minced ginger
2 cloves garlic, minced
2 tablespoons soy sauce
1 tablespoon toasted sesame seeds

SPICY HACK

Add 1 teaspoon of red pepper flakes or chili paste with the soy sauce in step 3.

STEPS

1. Bring a large pot of salted water to a rolling boil over high heat. Prepare an ice bath by putting cold water and ice in a large bowl.

2. Blanch the green beans by cooking them in the boiling water for 3 minutes. Drain the beans when the cooking time is up, and place them directly in the ice bath.

3. Place the pot back on the stove and add the sesame oil, minced garlic, and minced ginger. Turn the burner on medium-low heat and cook, stirring often, until garlic is fragrant and beginning to brown, about 3 minutes. Add the soy sauce and stir to combine.

4. Remove the pot from the heat. Drain the green beans and add them to the pot. Toss to coat the beans in the sauce.

5. Put the green beans on a plate or serving platter and sprinkle with sesame seeds.

Blanching and Ice Baths

To blanch vegetables, cook them in salted boiling water until they are just cooked through (but still slightly crisp). While they're cooking, fill a large bowl with ice water. Remove the vegetables from the boiling water and drop them into the ice bath. This will instantly stop them from cooking to maintain their texture and bright color. It's a method commonly used with green beans, spinach, asparagus, broccoli, and cauliflower.

LEMON POUND CAKE

Makes 8 generous servings.

INGREDIENTS
1½ cups all-purpose flour
¼ teaspoon baking soda
¼ teaspoon salt
½ cup butter (1 stick)
1 cup sugar
3 eggs
½ cup freshly squeezed lemon juice
½ cup sour cream
1 teaspoon vanilla extract
Optional: fresh fruit, honey

STEPS

1. Preheat the oven to 325°F.

2. Grease the sides and bottom of a loaf pan with butter and dust with flour. Tap the pan to spread the flour and make sure it coats the whole pan, then tap the pan upside down over the sink to remove any excess flour.

3. Sift the flour and baking soda into a medium bowl. Add the salt and stir to combine.

4. Beat butter with a mixer until fluffy. Add the sugar, ¼ cup at a time, and beat together for 5 minutes.

5. Add the eggs one at a time, mixing between each one to combine. Add the lemon juice and vanilla and mix to combine.

6. Add the dry ingredients in three parts, mixing to combine between each.

7. Add the sour cream, and mix until combined.

8. Pour the batter into a prepared loaf pan.

9. Bake for 60–70 minutes, until the top is light brown and a toothpick or sharp knife inserted into the center of the loaf comes out clean.

10. Remove from the oven and let cool in the pan for at least 20 minutes. Serve slices of cake drizzled with honey and topped with fresh fruit, if using.

GOURMET HACK

Serve with the berry dip on page 119. Substitute orange juice, blood orange juice, or Meyer lemon juice for the lemon.

Follow Directions

Always follow baking recipes closely, since the specific timing helps achieve the best result. Baking is a science, and instructions are included for a reason. As an example, beating the batter for 5 minutes in step 4 adds air to the butter-and-sugar mix and will make the lightest batter possible.

A Fancy Dinner

Scene: The kitchen in your new apartment. Flickering candlelight. Adele playing softly in the background.

The goal: Impress your date with a beautiful meal.

The Menu
French goat cheese salad
Herb braised pork
Herbed rice pilaf
Lemon pound cake

COMPANY HACK
Make the meal for your friends; they like to eat too! (Maybe switch out the Adele, depending on the crowd.)

TIME HACK
Make the pork and the cake the day before, to eliminate some of the stress of entertaining.

AFTERWORD

Throughout this book, we've focused on cooking and eating with friends because we truly believe that food tastes better when shared. Some of the recipes are variations of classics that we've learned from our own families and still cook regularly. This collaborative culinary experience has helped us create the variations and hacks indicated at the end of each recipe. We hope this book has given you confidence in the kitchen and the desire to experiment with new dishes and cuisines!

Just remember, learning to cook requires trial and error. Don't be discouraged if you burn a dish, your recipe is too salty, or the end result doesn't meet your expectations. Think about what you would change, and do it differently next time. Make notes on the recipes about what you learned, what you liked, and what you didn't like, to make sure the dish gets better every time you make it.

CARLA

ALYSSA

CONVERSION CHART

LIQUID/DRY MEASUREMENTS

US	Metric
1/4 teaspoon	1.25 milliliters
1/2 teaspoon	2.5 milliliters
1 teaspoon	5 milliliters
1 tablespoon (3 teaspoons)	15 milliliters
1 fluid ounce (2 tablespoons)	30 milliliters
1/4 cup	60 milliliters
1/3 cup	80 milliliters
1/2 cup	120 milliliters
1 cup	240 milliliters
1 pint (2 cups)	480 milliliters
1 quart (4 cups/32 ounces)	960 milliliters
1 gallon (4 quarts)	3.84 liters
1 ounce (by weight)	28 grams
1 pound	448 grams
2.2 pounds	1 kilogram

Note: Some measurements have been rounded.

COOKING TEMPERATURES

Fahrenheit	Celsius
250°	120°
275°	140°
300°	150°
325°	160°
350°	180°
375°	190°
400°	200°
425°	220°
450°	230°
475°	240°
500°	260°

INDEX

NOTES

We would like to thank all of our recipe testers and retesters. And we'd like to give a very special thank-you to Pam for her advice and help and, well, everything.
—C.C. and A.W.

Thanks to my mom for making me lots of cheesecake and thumbprint cookies and scrambled eggs and TWA, Angie's love of Carlamels, Cindy's hand-washing machine (I still think about it every day in the kitchen), and Laura's birthday pupusas. And should you ever have the opportunity to write a cookbook with your best friend, DO IT. Alyssa, you're the honey in my tea.
—C.C.

To the many people who have served as willing testers of my culinary experiments over the years: my entire family, my patient husband, our Tokyo crew, and my friends. To my parents, whom I cannot possibly thank enough for supporting so many creative projects over the years. To Gram: I wish you could brag about this book to everyone you know; you would be beyond thrilled. And to Carla: I so loved our caffeine-fueled marathon days of cooking and shooting this book! You're amazing.
—A.W.

Zest Books™
An imprint of Lerner Publishing Group, Inc.
241 First Avenue North
Minneapolis, MN 55401 USA

For reading levels and more information, look up this title at www.lernerbooks.com.
Visit us at zestbooks.net.

Main body text set in Avenir Next.
Typeface provided by Linotype AG.

Image credits: Shutterstock.com, pp. 2-9, 11, 47, 79, 123; QinJin/Shutterstock.com, pp. 14 & 15, 48 & 49, 80–83, 124–127. Additional Images: Alyssa Wiegand and Carla Carreon.

Library of Congress Cataloging-in-Publication Data
Names: Wiegand, Alyssa, 1984- author. | Carreon, Carla, 1981- author.
Title: Hack your cupboard : make great food with what you've got / by Alyssa Wiegand and Carla Carreon.
Description: Minneapolis : Zest Books, [2019] | Includes index. |
Identifiers: LCCN 2018061559 (print) | LCCN 2019000224 (ebook) | ISBN 9781541578555 (eb pdf) | ISBN 9781541578548 (lib. bdg. : alk. paper) | ISBN 9781942186076 (pbk. : alk. paper)
Subjects: LCSH: Low budget cooking. | Cooking (Leftovers) | LCGFT: Cookbooks.
Classification: LCC TX652 (ebook) | LCC TX652 .W375 2019 (print) |
    DDC 641.5/52—dc23

LC record available at https://lccn.loc.gov/2018061559

Manufactured in the United States of America
1-46975-47844-5/7/2019